D1272542

Graphic Medieval History

THE BLACK DEATH

By Gary Jeffrey & Illustrated by Alessandro Poluzzi

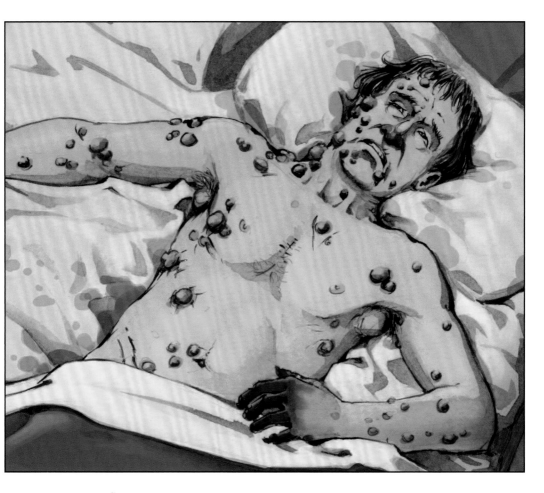

Crabtree Publishing Company
www.crabtreebooks.com

Crabtree Publishing Company
www.crabtreebooks.com
1-800-387-7650

Publishing in Canada
616 Welland Ave.
St. Catharines, ON
L2M 5V6

Published in the United States
PMB 59051, 350 Fifth Ave.
59th Floor,
New York, NY 10118

Published in **2014 by CRABTREE PUBLISHING COMPANY.**

Printed in Canada/032014/MA20140124

Created and produced by:
David West Children's Books

Project development, design, and concept:
David West Children's Books

Author and designer: Gary Jeffrey

Illustrator: Alessandro Poluzzi

Editor: Kathy Middleton

Proofreader: Adrianna Morganelli

Production coordinator and
  Prepress technician:
  Ken Wright

Print coordinator:
  Margaret Amy Salter

Photo credits:
  page 5t, National Media
  Museum, 5m, Otis Historicl
  Archives of National Museum
  of Health & Medicine; page 47,
  Jean-Pol GRANDMONT

Library and Archives Canada Cataloguing in Publication

Jeffrey, Gary, author
     The Black Death / Gary Jeffrey ; illustrator: Alessandro
Poluzzi.

(Graphic medieval history)
Includes index.
Issued in print and electronic formats.
ISBN 978-0-7787-0400-3 (bound).--ISBN 978-0-7787-0406-5
(pbk.).--ISBN 978-1-4271-7512-0 (html).--ISBN 978-1-4271-7518-2
(pdf)

     1. Black Death--Europe--Juvenile literature. 2. Black
Death--Europe--Comic books, strips, etc. 3. Graphic novels. I.
Poluzzi, Alessandro, illustrator II. Title. III. Series: Jeffrey, Gary.
Graphic medieval history.

RC178.A1J45 2014   j614.5'732   C2014-900365-X
                                                                      C2014-900366-8

Library of Congress Cataloging-in-Publication Data

Jeffrey, Gary, author.
 The black death / by Gary Jeffrey ; illustrated by Alessandro
Poluzzi.
      pages cm -- (Graphic medieval history)
 Includes index.
 ISBN 978-0-7787-0400-3 (reinforced library binding : alk.
paper) -- ISBN 978-0-7787-0406-5 (pbk. : alk. paper) -- ISBN
978-1-4271-7512-0 (electronic html) -- ISBN 978-1-4271-7518-2
(electronic pdf)
1. Plague--Europe--History--Juvenile literature. 2. Plague--
England--London--History--Juvenile literature. 3. Plague--
Europe--History--Comic books, strips, etc. 4. Plague--England-
-London--History--Comic books, strips, etc. 5. Graphic novels.
I. Poluzzi, Alessandro, illustrator. II. Title.

 RC178.A1J44 2015
 614.5'732094--dc23
                                                            2014002262

Contents

Black Death

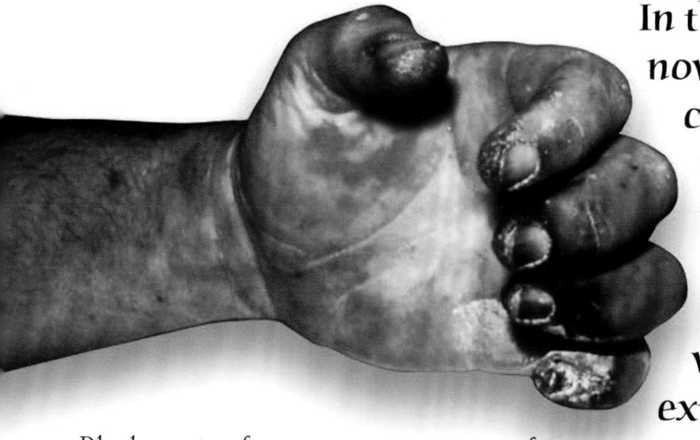

In the 1300s, from out of nowhere a deadly disease came that spread like wildfire and killed its unlucky victims within hours. Whole cities, even civilizations, were threatened with extinction by plague.

Black, rotting fingertips are symptoms of septicemic plague—a disease that infects the blood and, in medieval times, was always fatal.

First Outbreak

The disease first struck with great force in the spring of 542 CE in the city of Constantinople, in the eastern part of the Roman empire called Byzantium. The outbreak quickly spread across the whole empire, becoming the first recorded pandemic. The plague killed an estimated 25 million people and destroyed Roman emperor Justinian's hope of reclaiming lost lands to reestablish the western Roman empire.

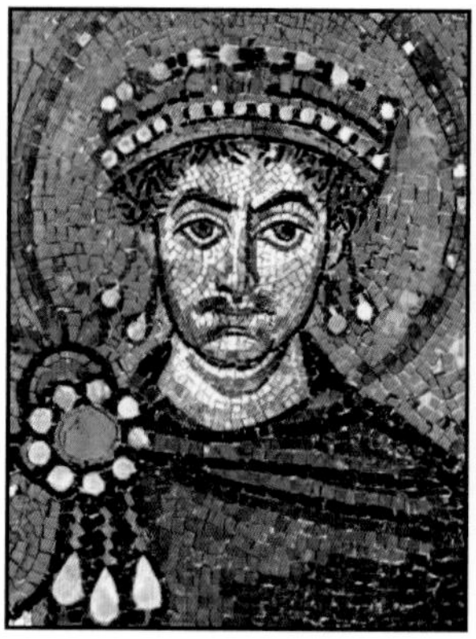

Emperor Justinian caught the first plague but survived. He went on to found the first legal system of justice.

Powerful Strain

Medieval doctors could not determine the cause of the plague. Today, we know the plague is caused by a bacteria that invades a body and multiplies, releasing toxins, or poisons. It was originally a disease that affected fleas on rodents. At first, it caused only mild, flu-like symptoms in humans. Over time, however, it changed into a deadly strain, or type—*Yersinia pestis*—the bubonic plague.

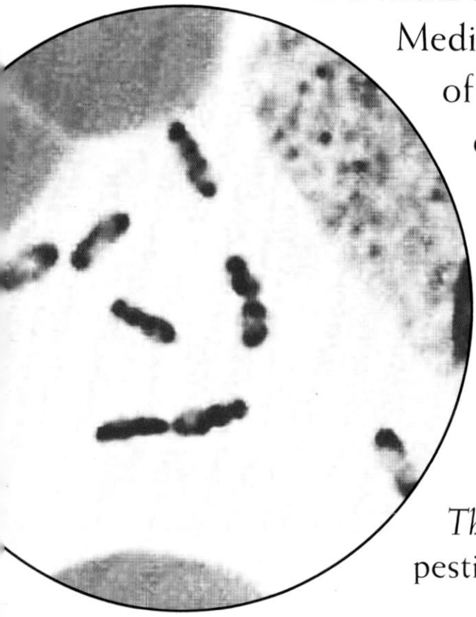

This microscopic view shows the plague bacteria, Yersinia pestis, *which has a shape like a paperclip.*

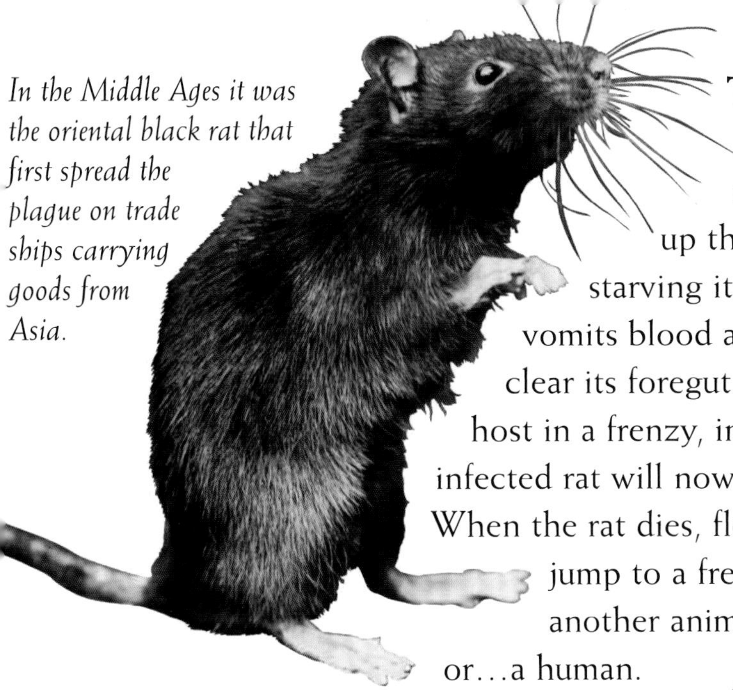

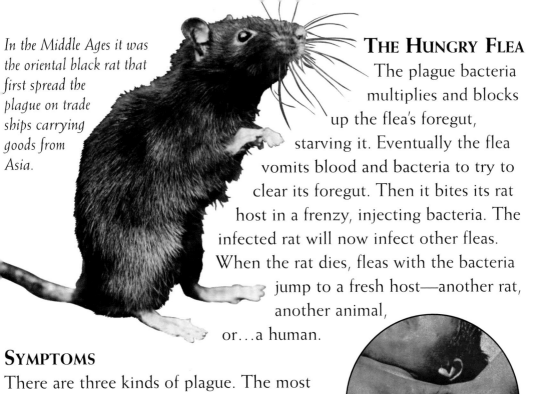

In the Middle Ages it was the oriental black rat that first spread the plague on trade ships carrying goods from Asia.

The Hungry Flea

The plague bacteria multiplies and blocks up the flea's foregut, starving it. Eventually the flea vomits blood and bacteria to try to clear its foregut. Then it bites its rat host in a frenzy, injecting bacteria. The infected rat will now infect other fleas. When the rat dies, fleas with the bacteria jump to a fresh host—another rat, another animal, or…a human.

Symptoms

There are three kinds of plague. The most common, bubonic, attacks the lymph glands. Other types are septicemic, which causes infection of blood vessels, or pneumonic, which destroys the lungs and can be spread between people by their breath. Plague begins with fever and chills. Then terrible pain is felt as the sufferer's skin turns black at the extremities and rots.

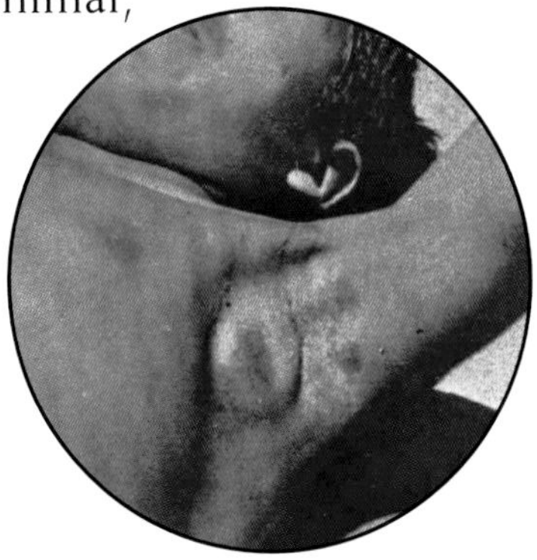

Swollen lymph glands called buboes are a sign of plague infection.

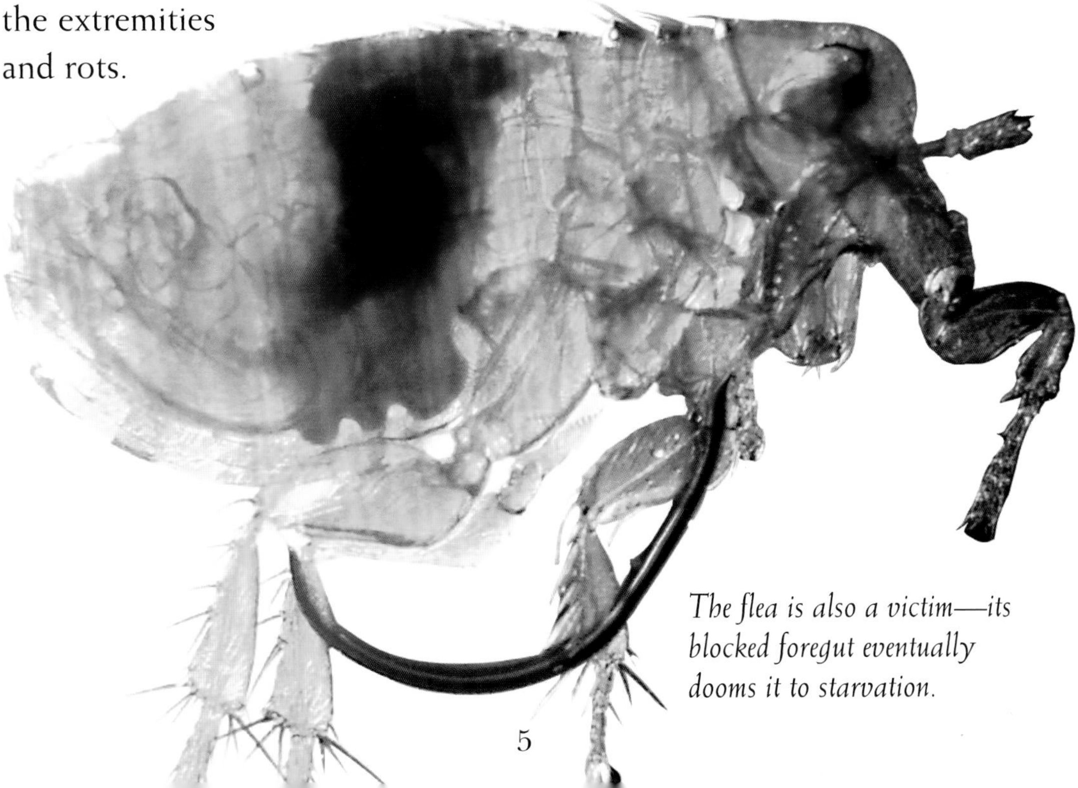

The flea is also a victim—its blocked foregut eventually dooms it to starvation.

Plague Routes

From the 11th century onward, the population of Europe exploded as great areas of wilderness were settled. Because of the huge numbers of people available to work, wages were low, and labor was cheap. The peasants stayed very poor. In the early 14th century, widespread starvation from failed harvests was an early taste of the disaster to come.

A woman goes hungry in the flames of the underworld in artwork made during the great famine of 1315–1317.

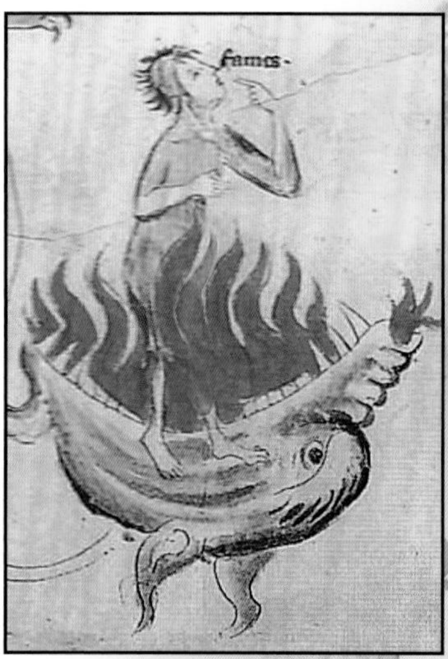
fames

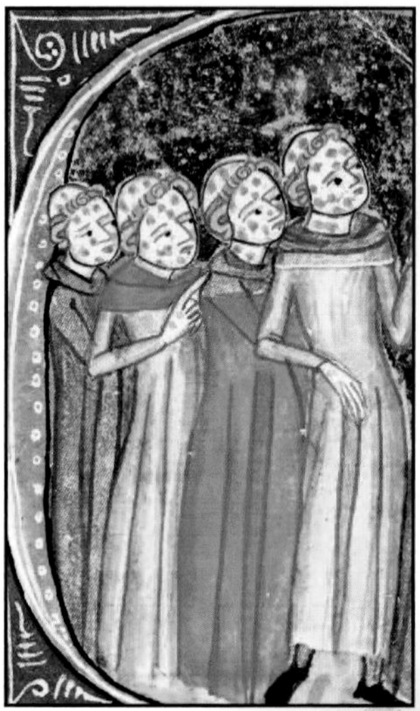

An illuminated manuscript shows disease-ridden monks. The close-knit inhabitants of monasteries, where the monks lived, were badly hit by the plague.

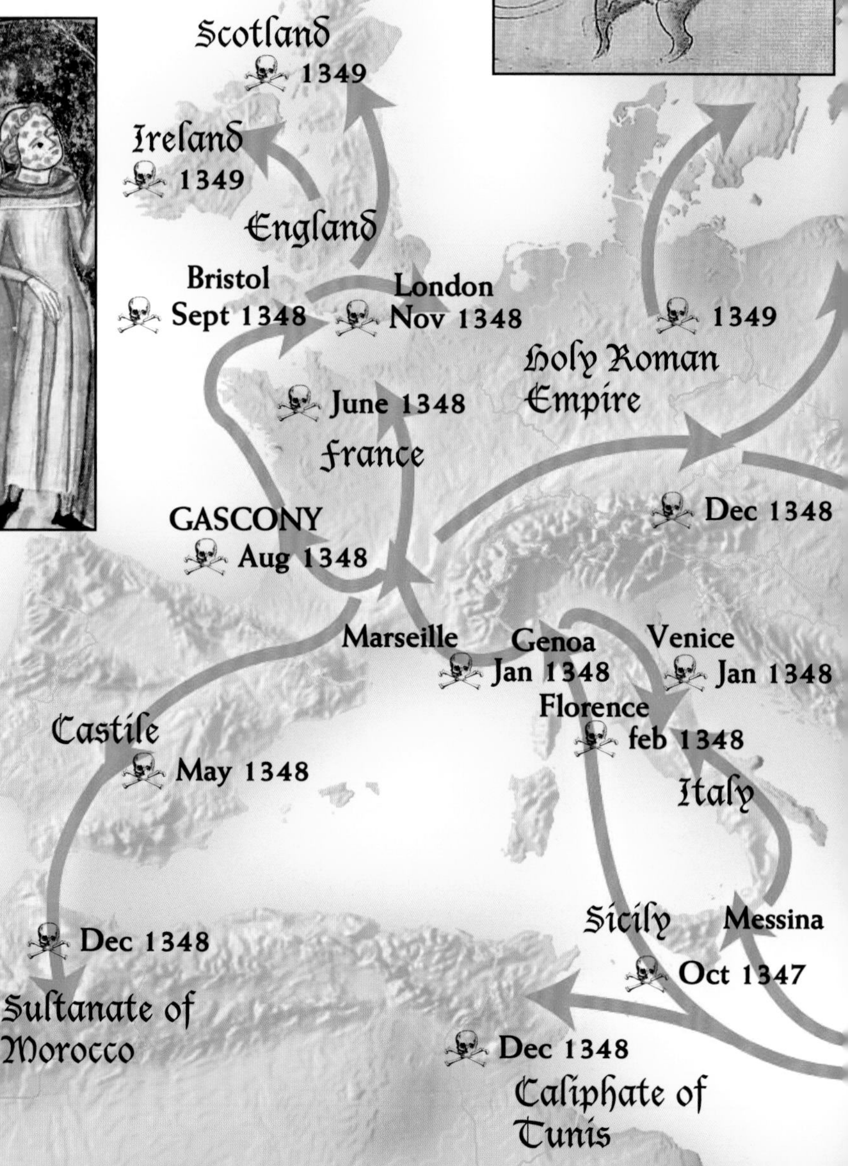
Scotland
1349
Ireland
1349
England
Bristol
Sept 1348
London
Nov 1348
1349
Holy Roman
Empire
June 1348
France
Dec 1348
GASCONY
Aug 1348
Marseille
Genoa
Jan 1348
Venice
Jan 1348
Florence
feb 1348
Italy
Castile
May 1348
Sicily
Messina
Oct 1347
Dec 1348
Sultanate of
Morocco
Dec 1348
Caliphate of
Tunis

Cutting a Swathe

The 1340s plague outbreak probably started in China and traveled west along the Silk Road, the trade route from Asia to Europe. The Italian city-states of Genoa and Venice had recently opened up trade routes across the Black Sea and were fighting with the Mongols of the Golden Horde when the plague struck the Genoese-ruled city of Kaffa (see page 8). Ships carried the pestilence, or deadly disease, back to Italy, where it wiped out over half of Venice and Florence (see page 18). The plague probably entered France through Marseilles and tore its way north and west, reaching England in September, 1348. The bubonic form could be survived if the buboes were lanced, and some of the population were naturally immune to it. But the disease killed rapidly, and the number of deaths was staggering.

The plague made its way to Scotland, Ireland, Germany, Russia, and even Scandinavia, as well as North Africa and the Middle East. By 1350, the population of Europe had been reduced by one-third.

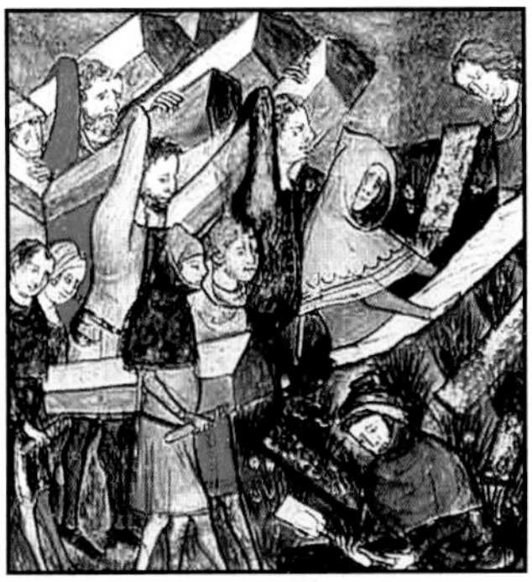

This 14th-century image shows plague victims being buried.

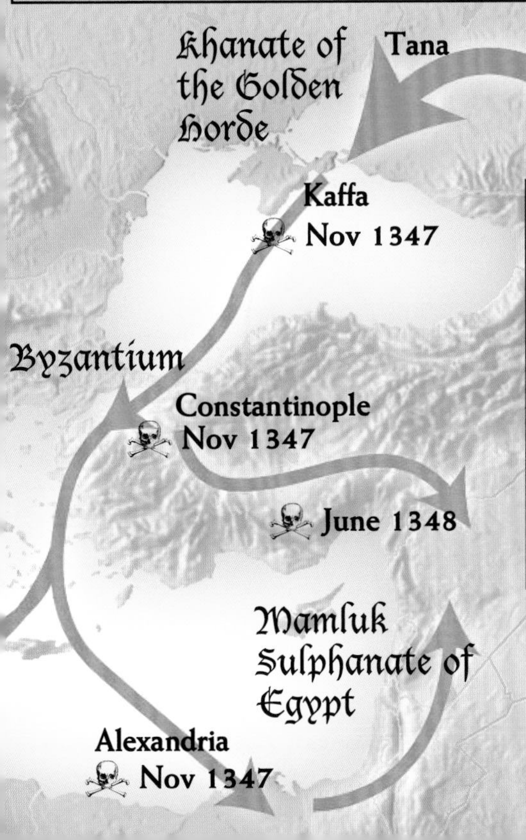
Khanate of the Golden Horde
Tana
Kaffa
Nov 1347
Byzantium
Constantinople
Nov 1347
June 1348
Mamluk Sulphanate of Egypt
Alexandria
Nov 1347

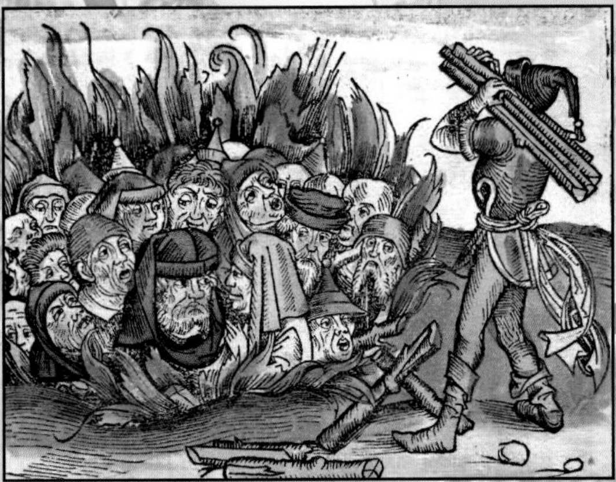

At first Jews were blamed for the calamity and many were burned, until the Pope ordered an end to their oppression in the summer of 1348.

How the Plague Came to Europe

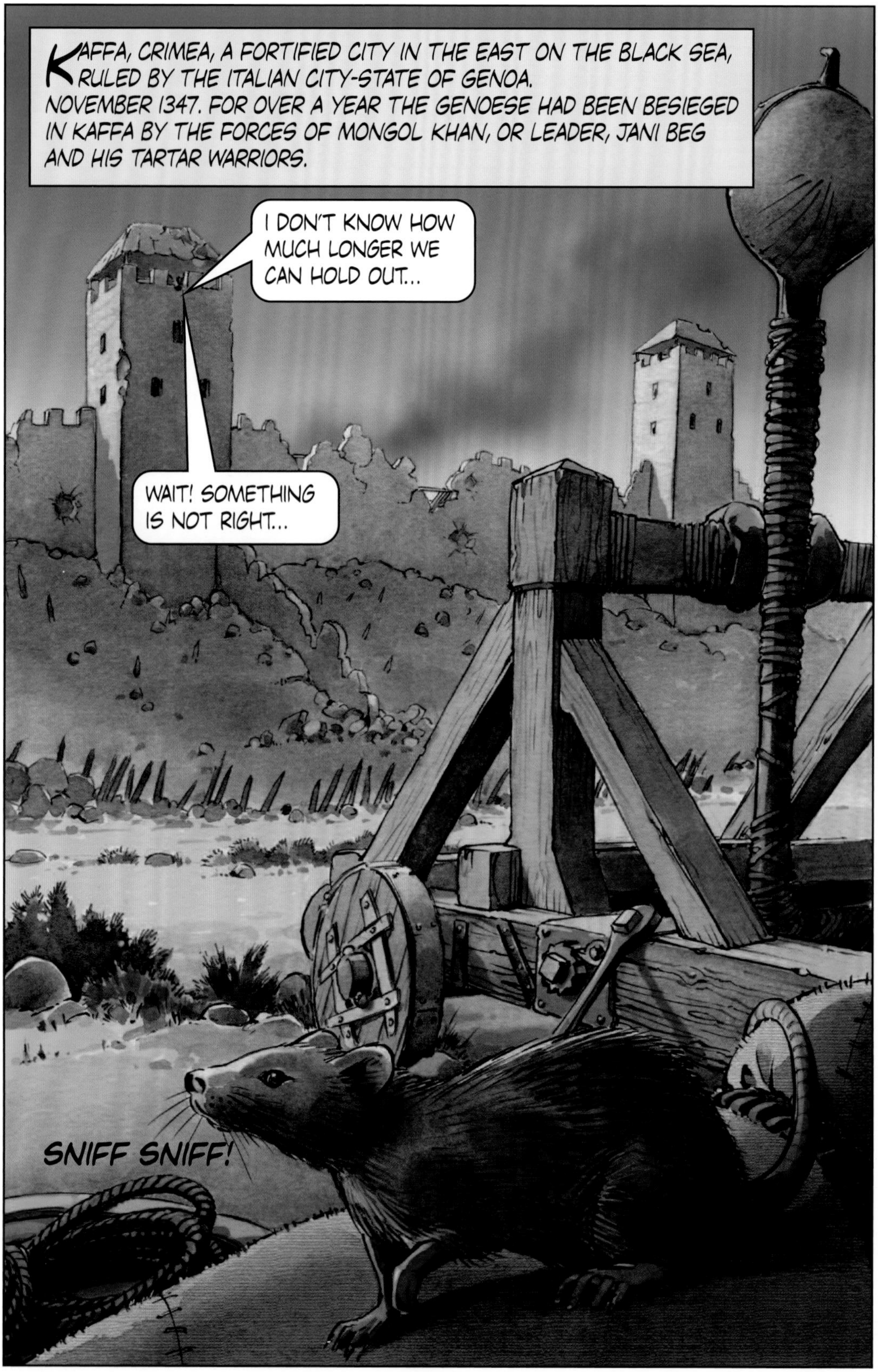

KAFFA, CRIMEA, A FORTIFIED CITY IN THE EAST ON THE BLACK SEA, RULED BY THE ITALIAN CITY-STATE OF GENOA.
NOVEMBER 1347. FOR OVER A YEAR THE GENOESE HAD BEEN BESIEGED IN KAFFA BY THE FORCES OF MONGOL KHAN, OR LEADER, JANI BEG AND HIS TARTAR WARRIORS.
I DON'T KNOW HOW MUCH LONGER WE CAN HOLD OUT...
WAIT! SOMETHING IS NOT RIGHT...
SNIFF SNIFF!

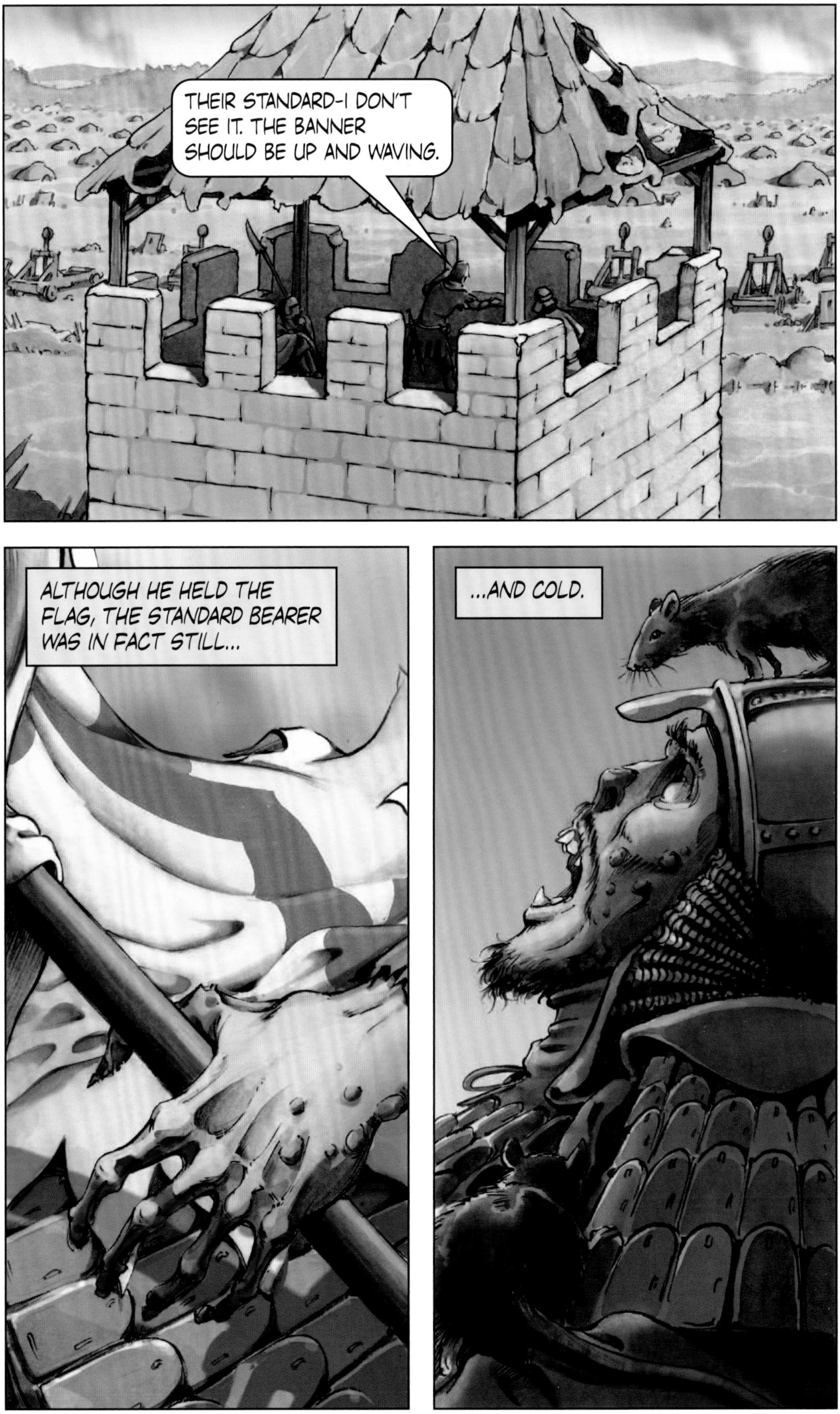
THEIR STANDARD-I DON'T SEE IT. THE BANNER SHOULD BE UP AND WAVING.
ALTHOUGH HE HELD THE FLAG, THE STANDARD BEARER WAS IN FACT STILL...
...AND COLD.

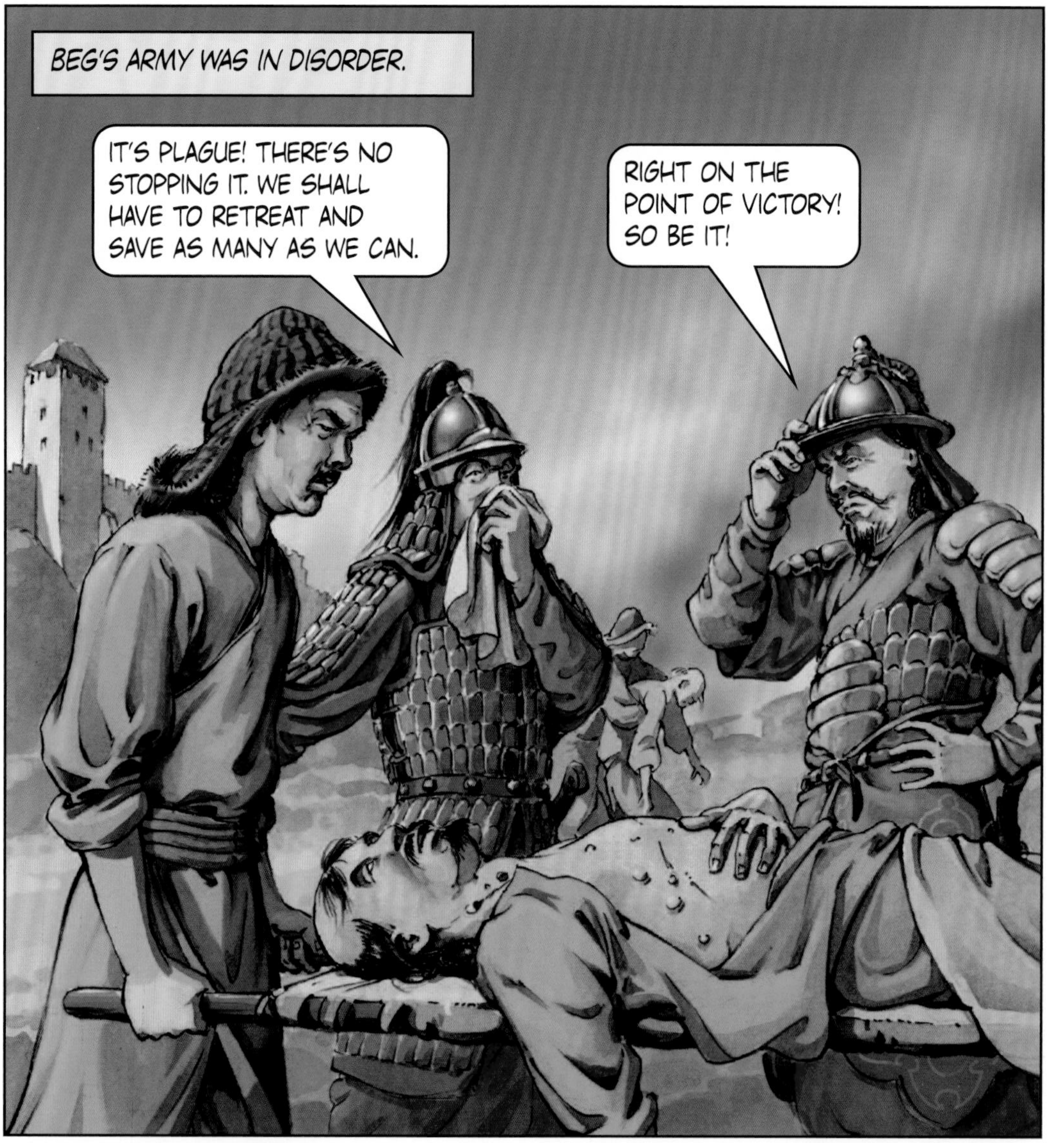
BEG'S ARMY WAS IN DISORDER.
IT'S PLAGUE! THERE'S NO STOPPING IT. WE SHALL HAVE TO RETREAT AND SAVE AS MANY AS WE CAN.
RIGHT ON THE POINT OF VICTORY! SO BE IT!

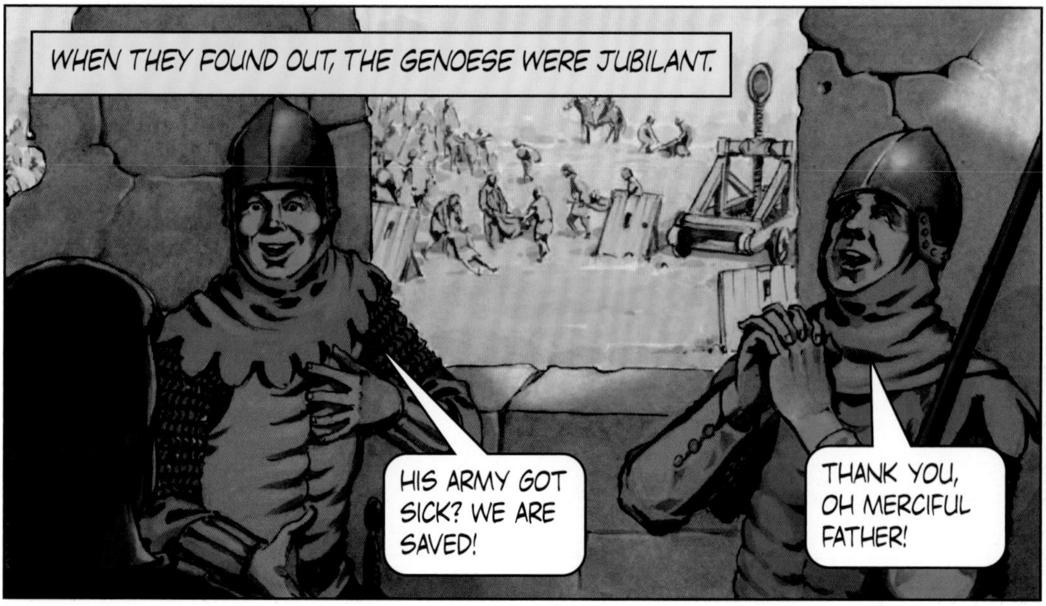
WHEN THEY FOUND OUT, THE GENOESE WERE JUBILANT.
HIS ARMY GOT SICK? WE ARE SAVED!
THANK YOU, OH MERCIFUL FATHER!

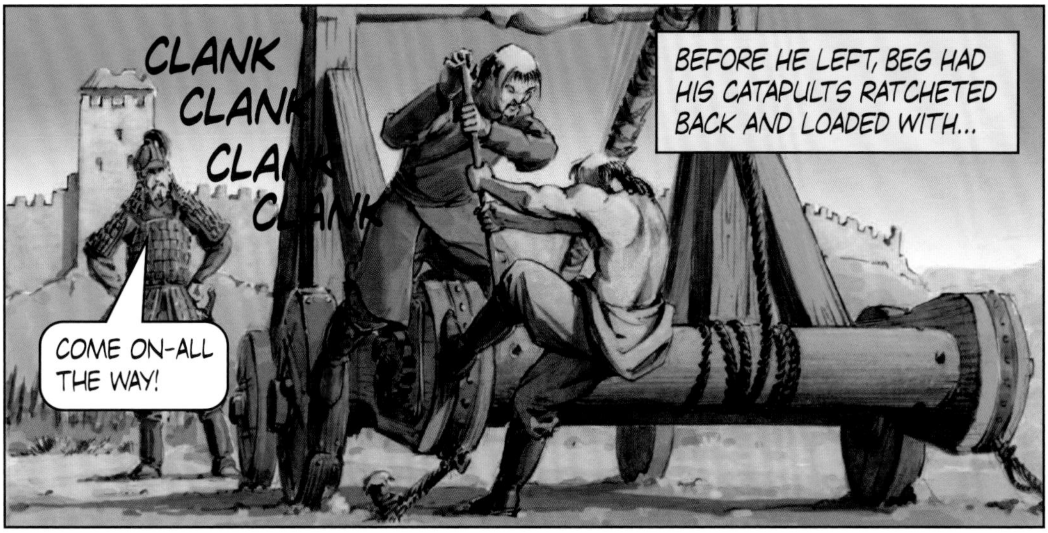
CLANK
CLANK
CLANK
CLANK
BEFORE HE LEFT, BEG HAD HIS CATAPULTS RATCHETED BACK AND LOADED WITH...
COME ON-ALL THE WAY!

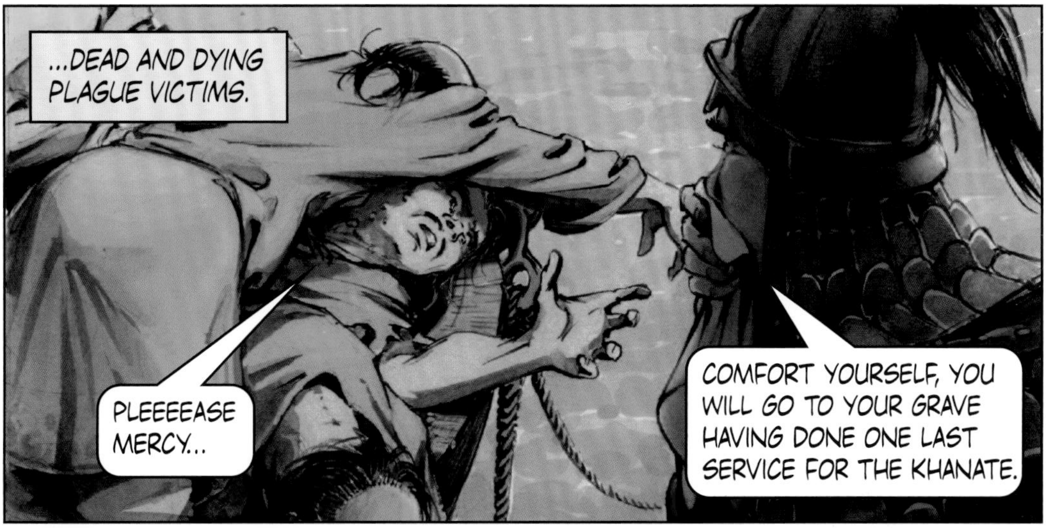
...DEAD AND DYING PLAGUE VICTIMS.
PLEEEEASE MERCY...
COMFORT YOURSELF, YOU WILL GO TO YOUR GRAVE HAVING DONE ONE LAST SERVICE FOR THE KHANATE.

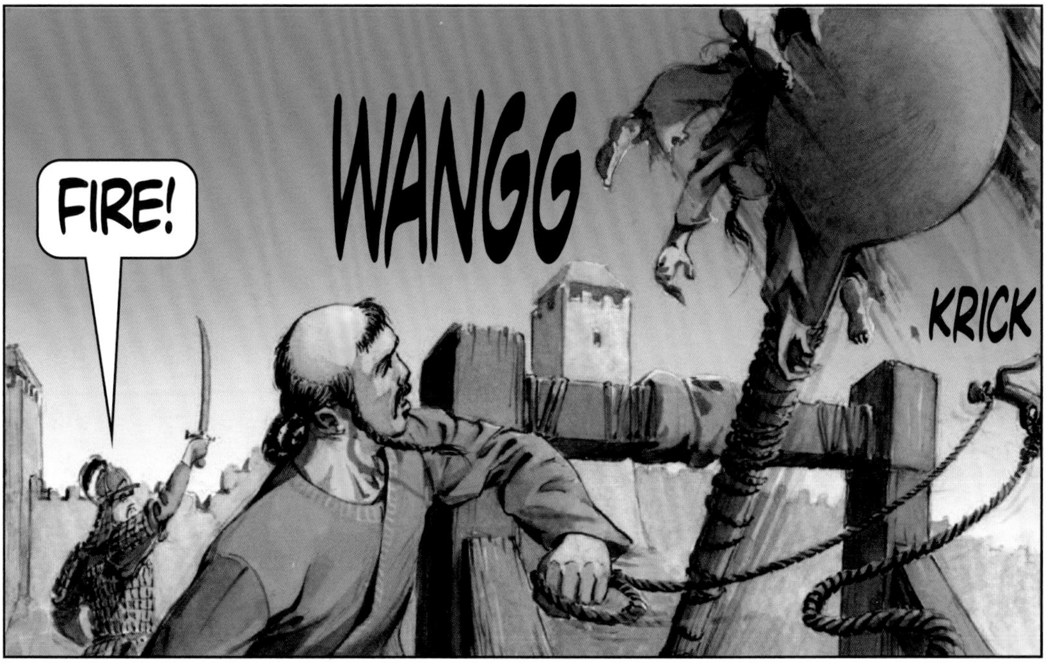
WANGG
FIRE!
KRICK

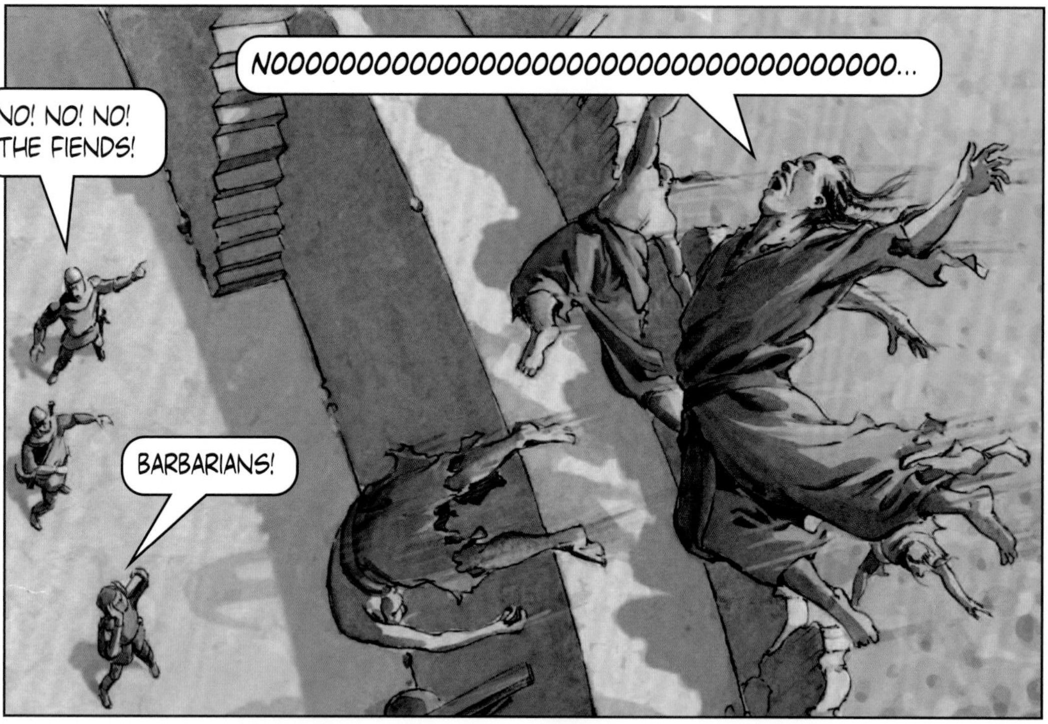
NO! NO! NO! THE FIENDS!
NOOOOOOOOOOOOOOOOOOOOOOOOOOOOOOOOOOOOOOOO...
BARBARIANS!

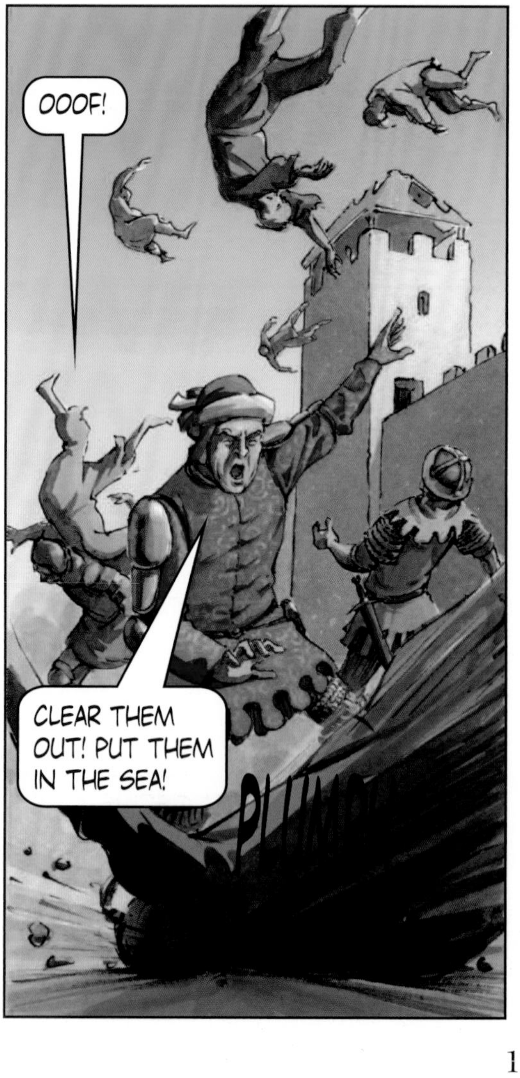
OOOF!
CLEAR THEM OUT! PUT THEM IN THE SEA!

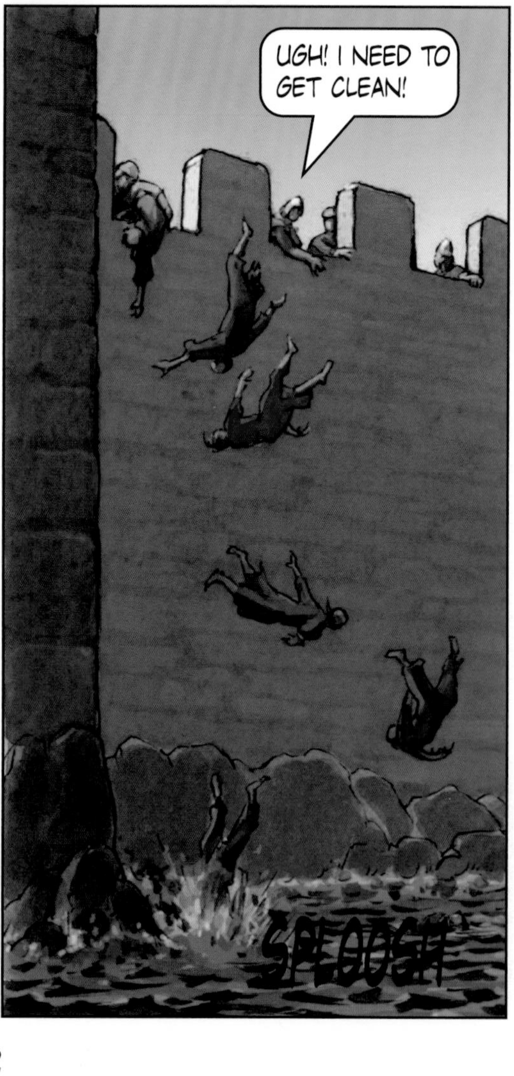
UGH! I NEED TO GET CLEAN!
SPLOOSH

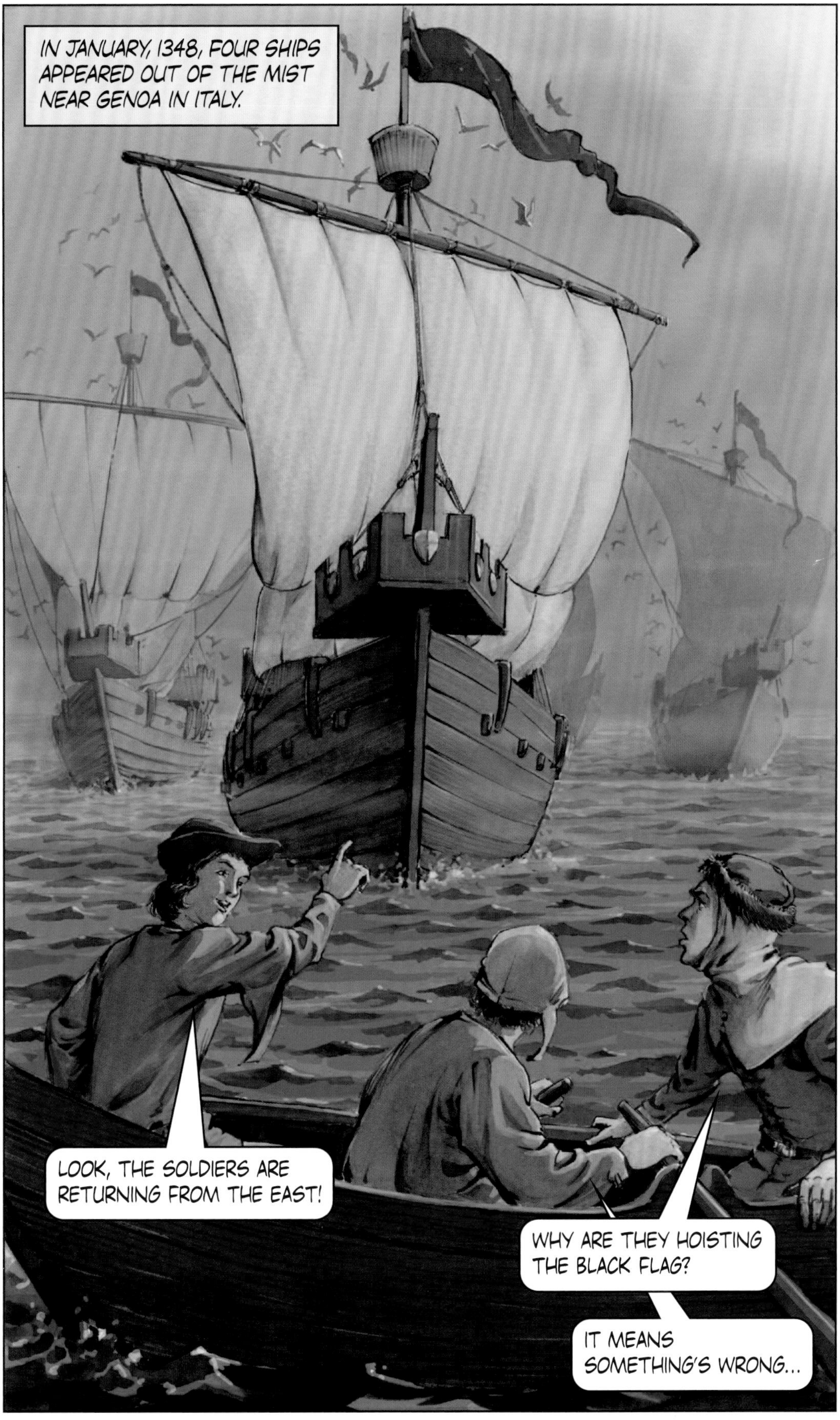

IN JANUARY, 1348, FOUR SHIPS APPEARED OUT OF THE MIST NEAR GENOA IN ITALY.
LOOK, THE SOLDIERS ARE RETURNING FROM THE EAST!
WHY ARE THEY HOISTING THE BLACK FLAG?
IT MEANS SOMETHING'S WRONG...

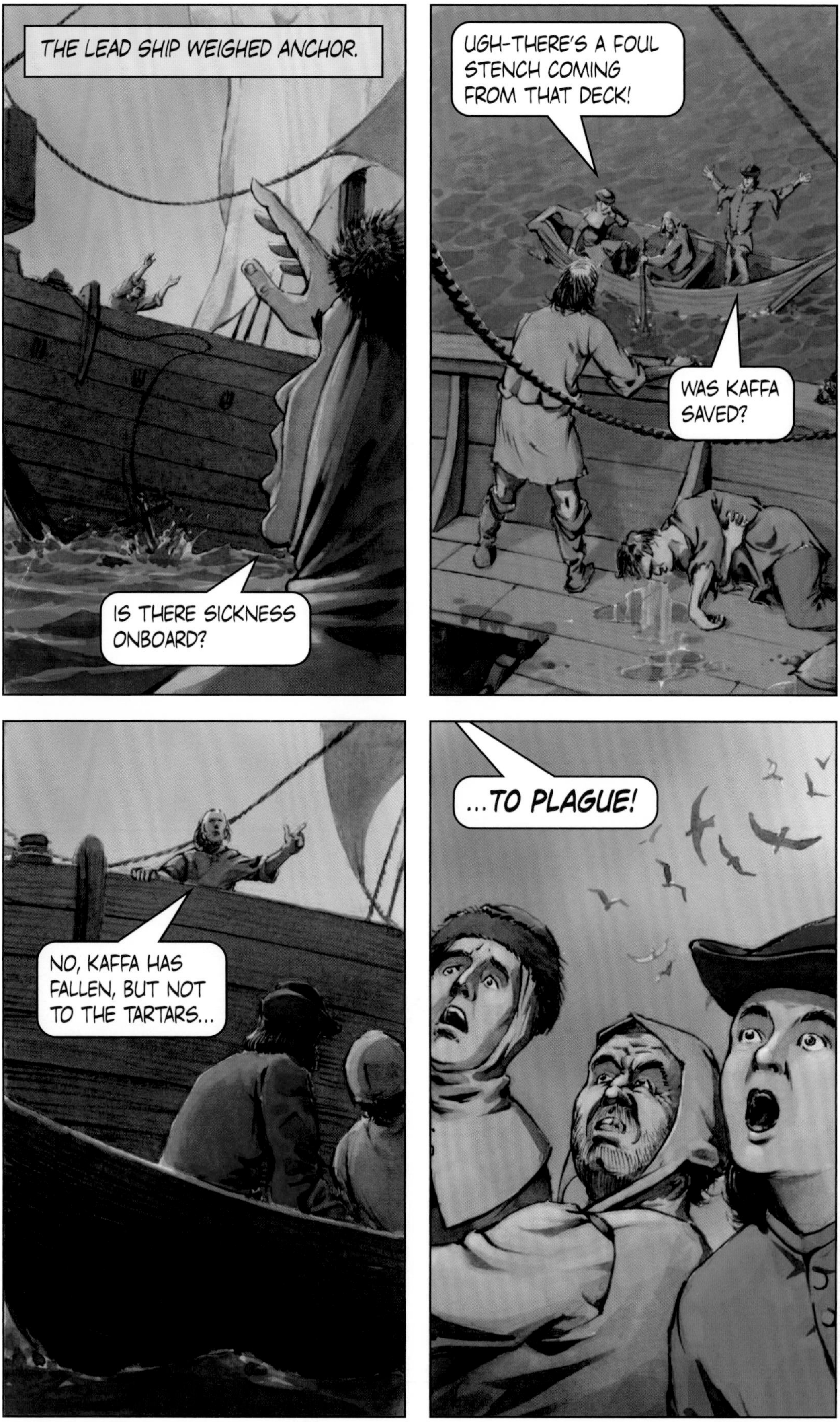
THE LEAD SHIP WEIGHED ANCHOR.
IS THERE SICKNESS ONBOARD?
UGH-THERE'S A FOUL STENCH COMING FROM THAT DECK!
WAS KAFFA SAVED?
NO, KAFFA HAS FALLEN, BUT NOT TO THE TARTARS...
...TO PLAGUE!

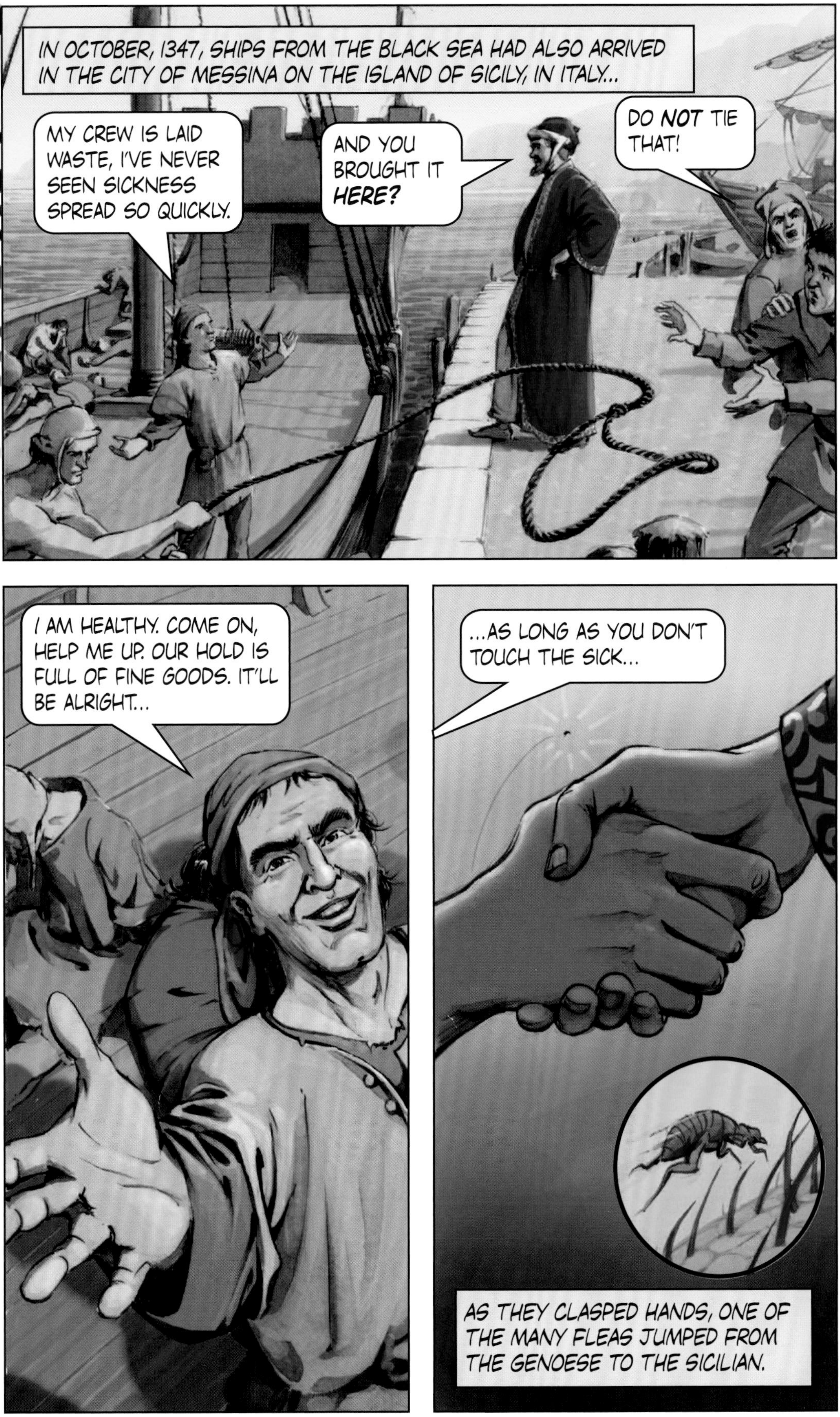
IN OCTOBER, 1347, SHIPS FROM THE BLACK SEA HAD ALSO ARRIVED IN THE CITY OF MESSINA ON THE ISLAND OF SICILY, IN ITALY...
MY CREW IS LAID WASTE, I'VE NEVER SEEN SICKNESS SPREAD SO QUICKLY.
AND YOU BROUGHT IT **HERE?**
DO **NOT** TIE THAT!
I AM HEALTHY. COME ON, HELP ME UP. OUR HOLD IS FULL OF FINE GOODS. IT'LL BE ALRIGHT...
...AS LONG AS YOU DON'T TOUCH THE SICK...
AS THEY CLASPED HANDS, ONE OF THE MANY FLEAS JUMPED FROM THE GENOESE TO THE SICILIAN.

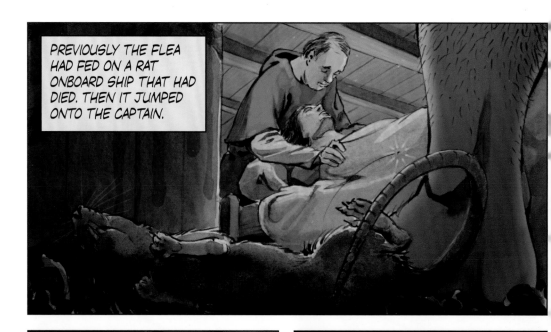

PREVIOUSLY THE FLEA HAD FED ON A RAT ONBOARD SHIP THAT HAD DIED. THEN IT JUMPED ONTO THE CAPTAIN.

BLOOD AND PLAGUE BACTERIA HAD BLOCKED THE FLEA'S GUT, STOPPING IT FROM FEEDING.

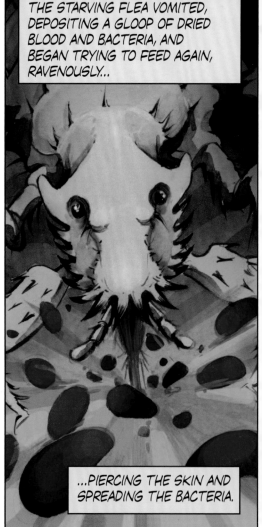

NOW ON THE SICILIAN'S SKIN, THE STARVING FLEA VOMITED, DEPOSITING A GLOOP OF DRIED BLOOD AND BACTERIA, AND BEGAN TRYING TO FEED AGAIN, RAVENOUSLY...

...PIERCING THE SKIN AND SPREADING THE BACTERIA.

THE NEXT DAY, THE CAPTAIN HIMSELF SUFFERED A RAGING FEVER AND SEVERE PAIN.

HE CAN'T TRAVEL LIKE THIS.

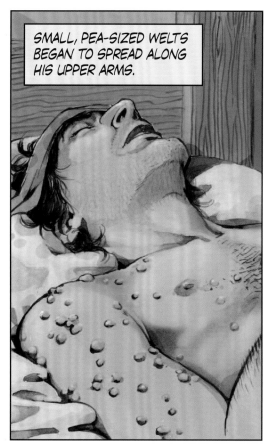

SMALL, PEA-SIZED WELTS BEGAN TO SPREAD ALONG HIS UPPER ARMS.

ON THE SECOND DAY, HE BEGAN COUGHING UP BLOOD.

HUERRK!

ON THE THIRD DAY, HE WAS DEAD.

NOT ONLY HAD HE HELPED BRING BUBONIC PLAGUE TO ITALY, HE HAD SPREAD PNEUMONIC PLAGUE AS WELL.

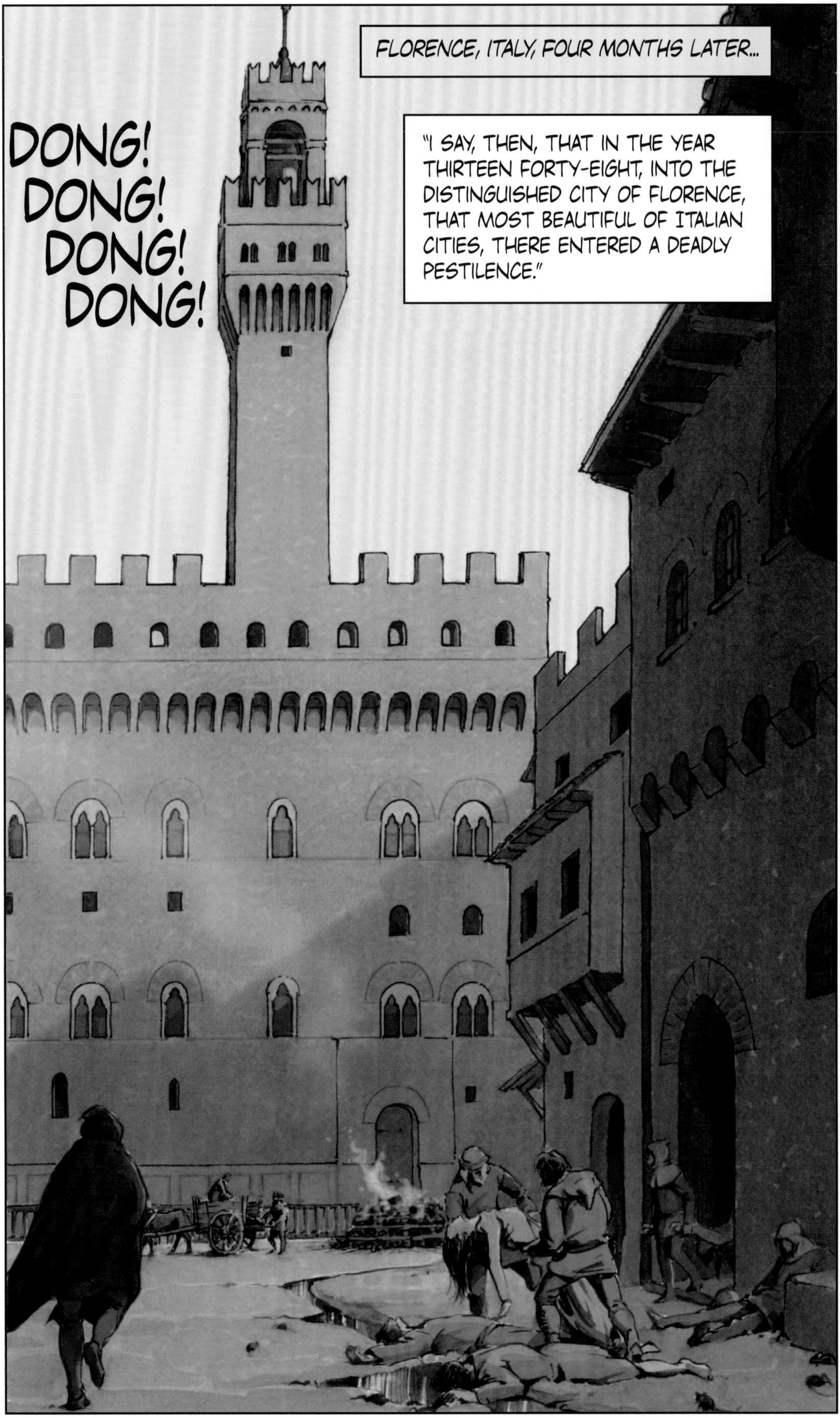
FLORENCE, ITALY, FOUR MONTHS LATER...
DONG! DONG! DONG! DONG!
"I SAY, THEN, THAT IN THE YEAR THIRTEEN FORTY-EIGHT, INTO THE DISTINGUISHED CITY OF FLORENCE, THAT MOST BEAUTIFUL OF ITALIAN CITIES, THERE ENTERED A DEADLY PESTILENCE."

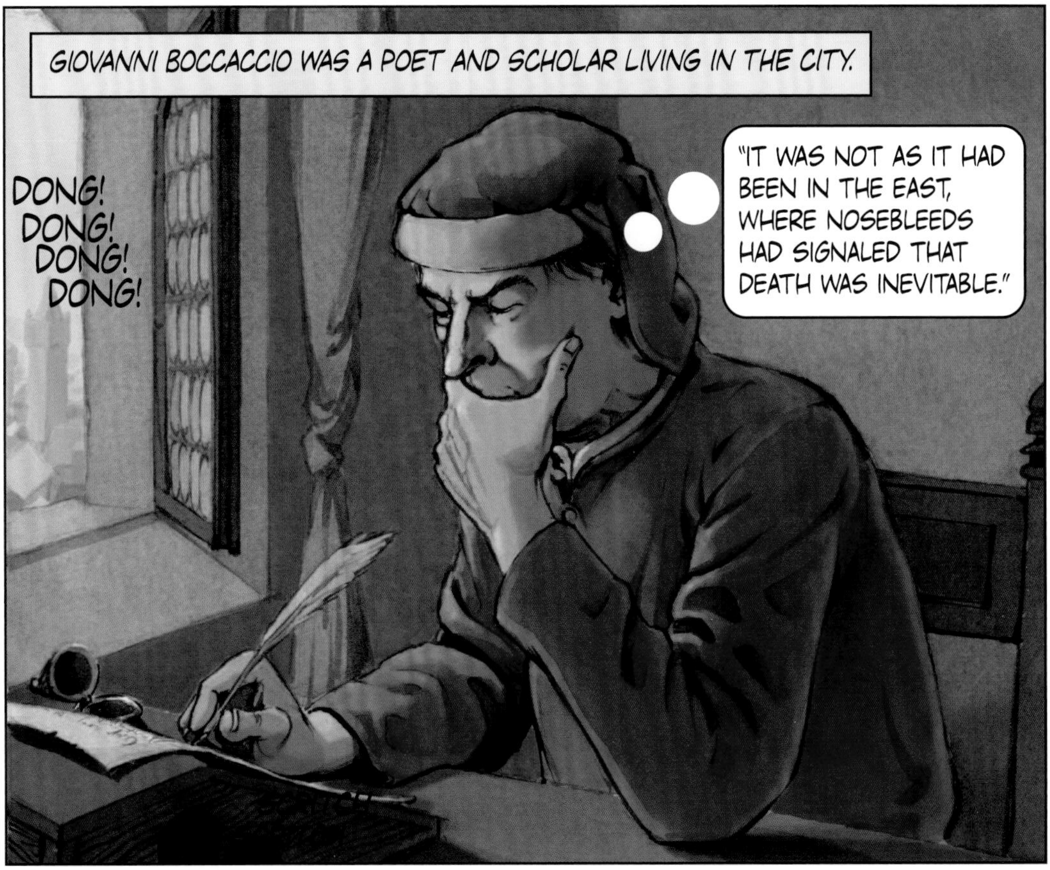
GIOVANNI BOCCACCIO WAS A POET AND SCHOLAR LIVING IN THE CITY.
DONG! DONG! DONG! DONG!
"IT WAS NOT AS IT HAD BEEN IN THE EAST, WHERE NOSEBLEEDS HAD SIGNALED THAT DEATH WAS INEVITABLE."

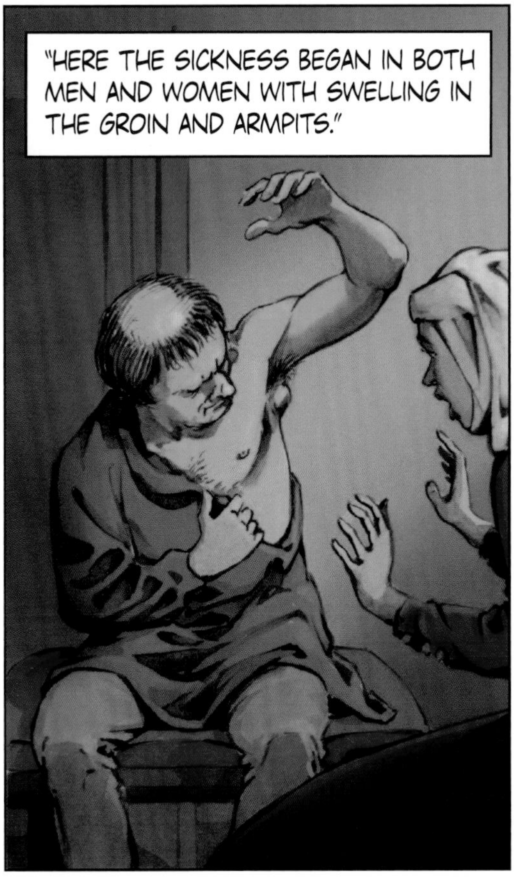
"HERE THE SICKNESS BEGAN IN BOTH MEN AND WOMEN WITH SWELLING IN THE GROIN AND ARMPITS."

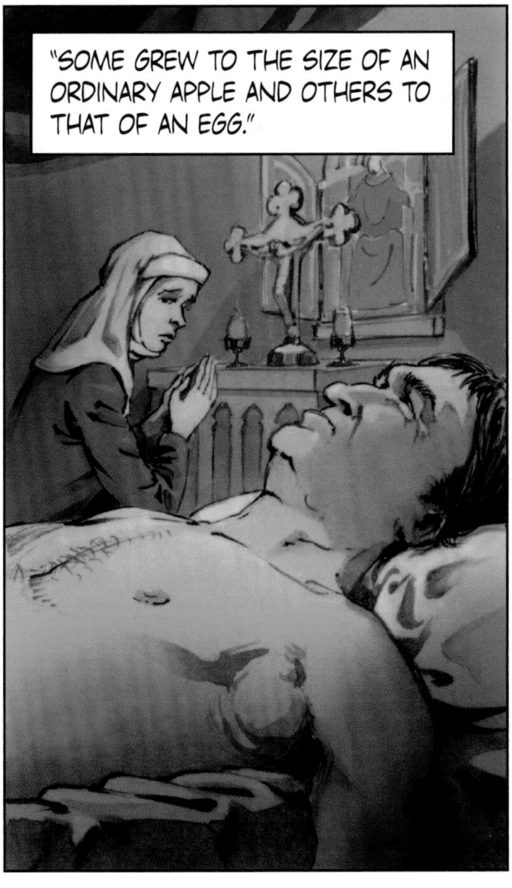
"SOME GREW TO THE SIZE OF AN ORDINARY APPLE AND OTHERS TO THAT OF AN EGG."

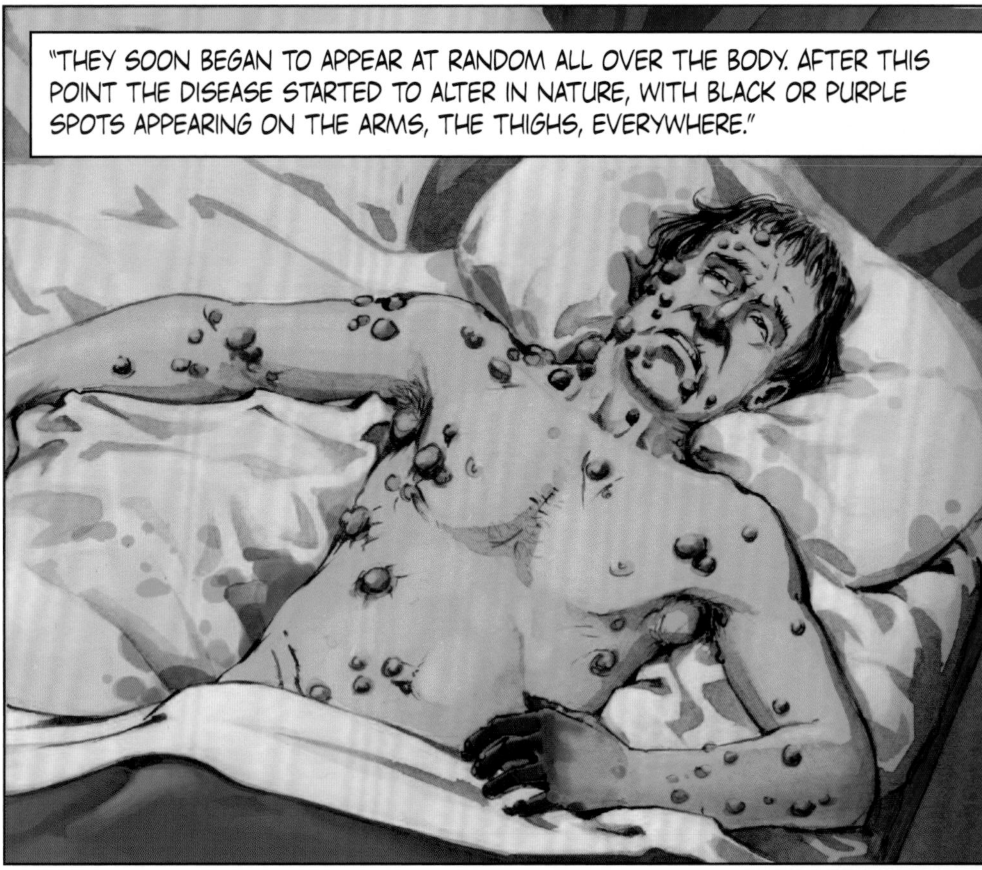
"THEY SOON BEGAN TO APPEAR AT RANDOM ALL OVER THE BODY. AFTER THIS POINT THE DISEASE STARTED TO ALTER IN NATURE, WITH BLACK OR PURPLE SPOTS APPEARING ON THE ARMS, THE THIGHS, EVERYWHERE."

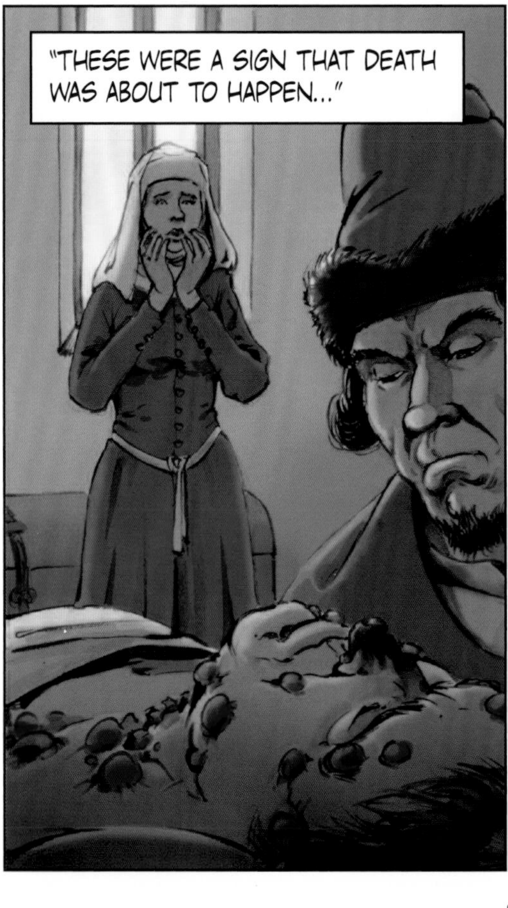
"THESE WERE A SIGN THAT DEATH WAS ABOUT TO HAPPEN..."

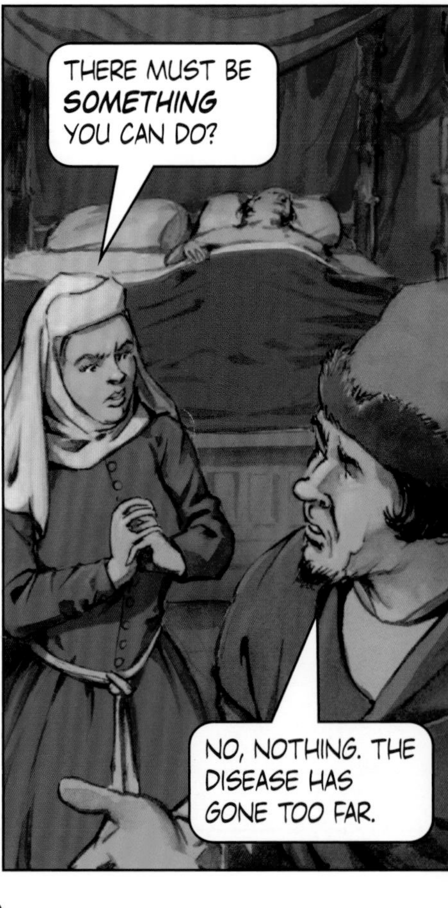
THERE MUST BE **SOMETHING** YOU CAN DO?
NO, NOTHING. THE DISEASE HAS GONE TOO FAR.

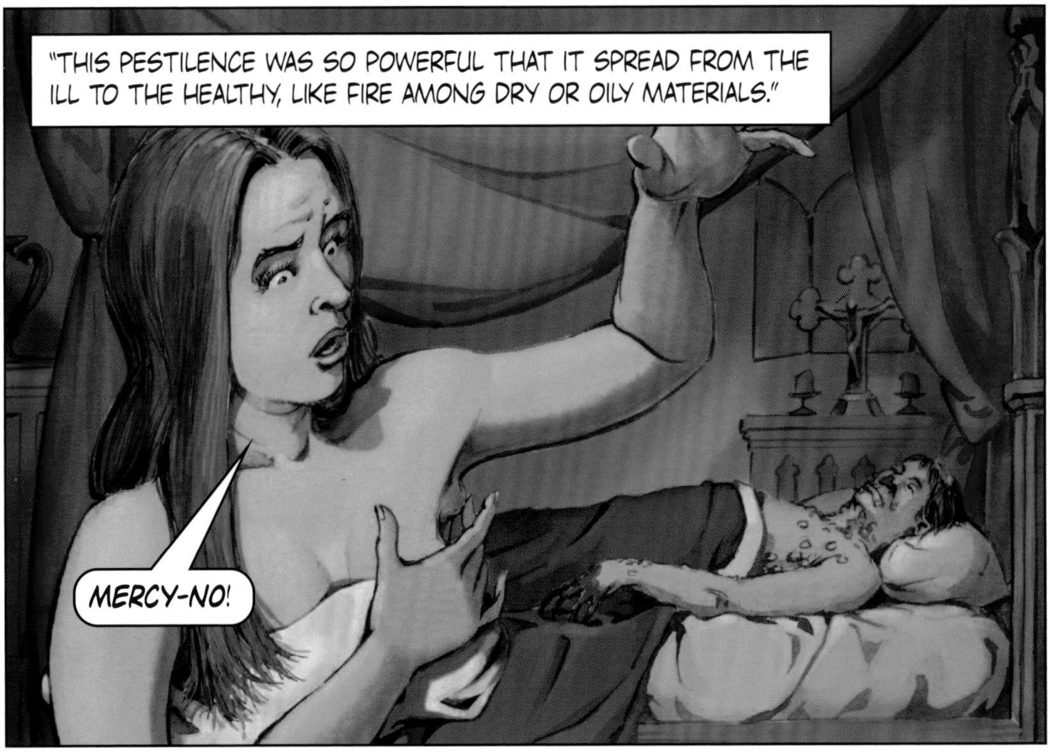
"THIS PESTILENCE WAS SO POWERFUL THAT IT SPREAD FROM THE ILL TO THE HEALTHY, LIKE FIRE AMONG DRY OR OILY MATERIALS."
MERCY-NO!

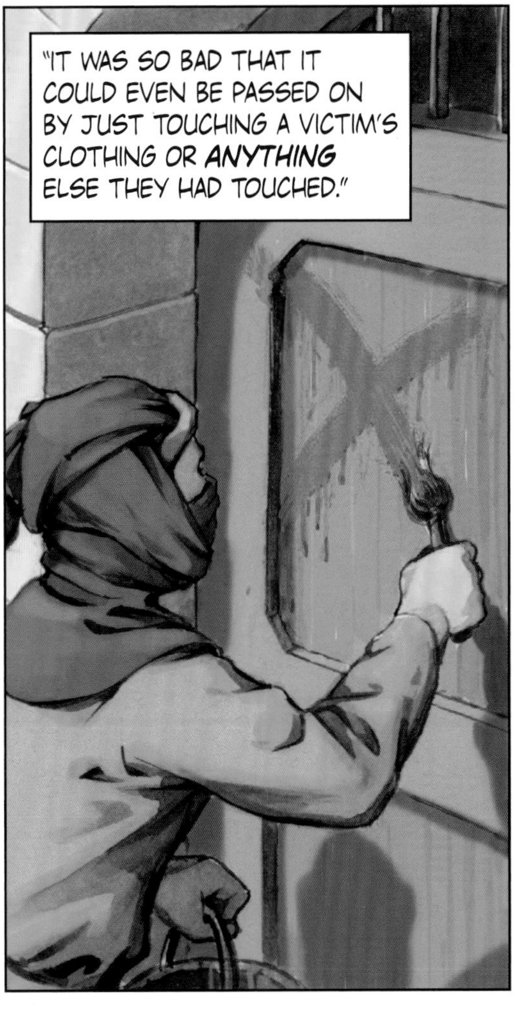
"IT WAS SO BAD THAT IT COULD EVEN BE PASSED ON BY JUST TOUCHING A VICTIM'S CLOTHING OR ANYTHING ELSE THEY HAD TOUCHED."

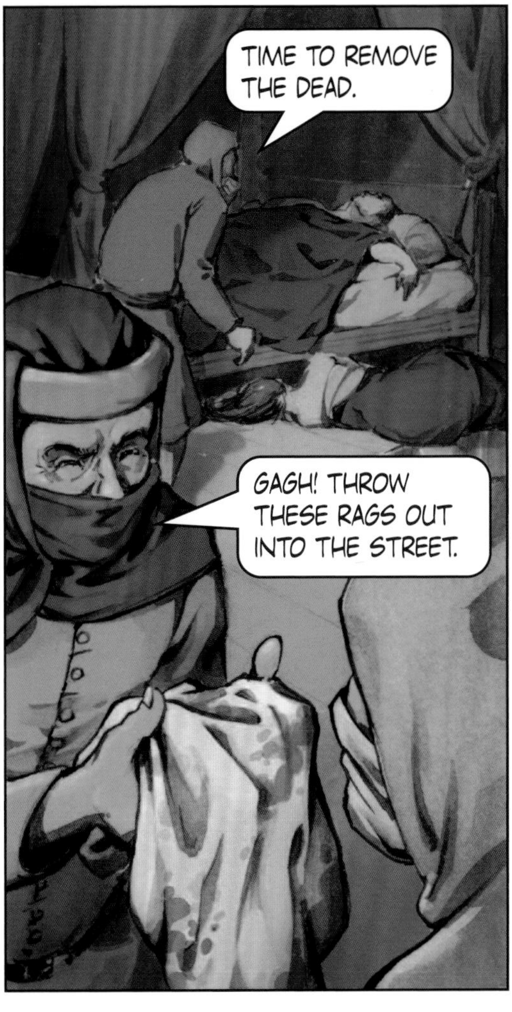
TIME TO REMOVE THE DEAD.
GAGH! THROW THESE RAGS OUT INTO THE STREET.

"IT SPREAD SO EASILY THAT, NOT ONLY DID IT PASS FROM PERSON TO PERSON, BUT IF AN ANIMAL TOUCHED THE BELONGINGS OF SOME SICK OR DEAD PERSON..."

OINK!

SNUFFLE

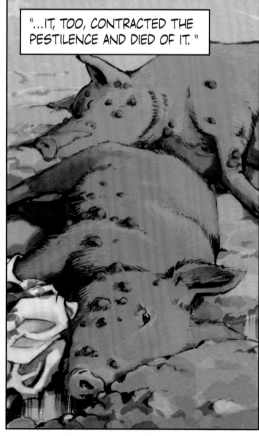

"...IT, TOO, CONTRACTED THE PESTILENCE AND DIED OF IT."

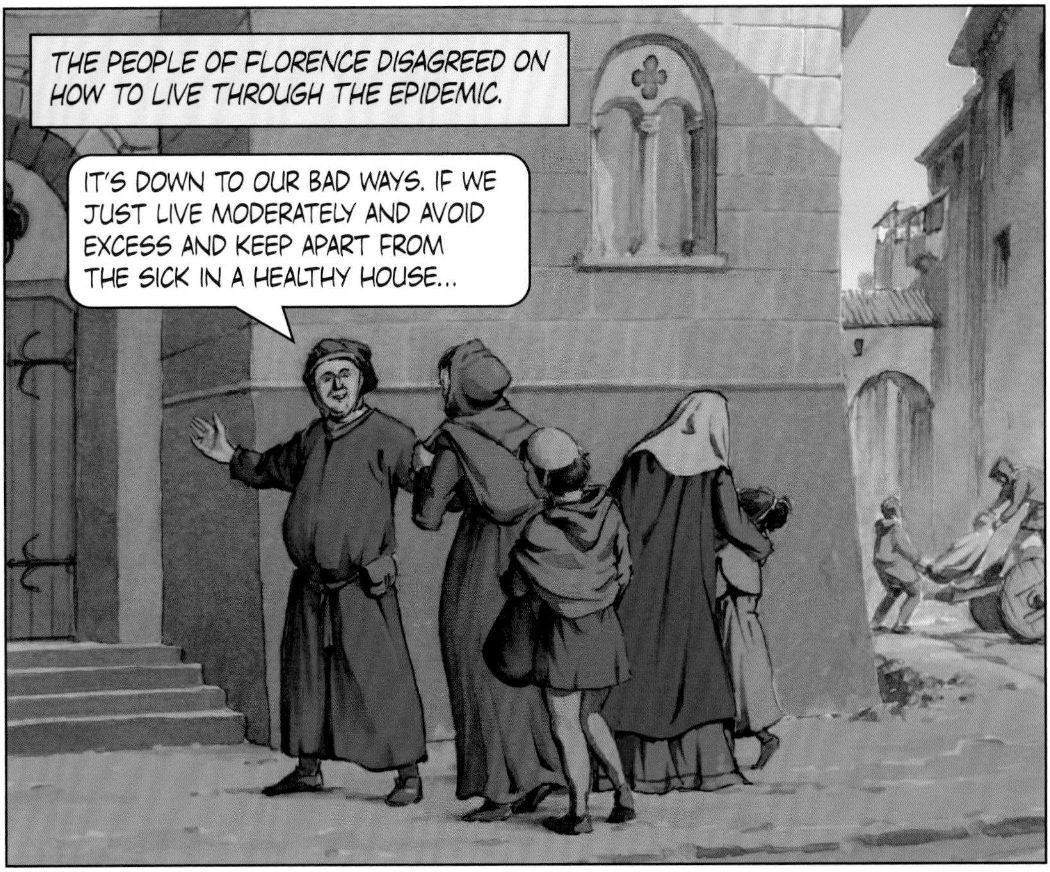
THE PEOPLE OF FLORENCE DISAGREED ON HOW TO LIVE THROUGH THE EPIDEMIC.
IT'S DOWN TO OUR BAD WAYS. IF WE JUST LIVE MODERATELY AND AVOID EXCESS AND KEEP APART FROM THE SICK IN A HEALTHY HOUSE...

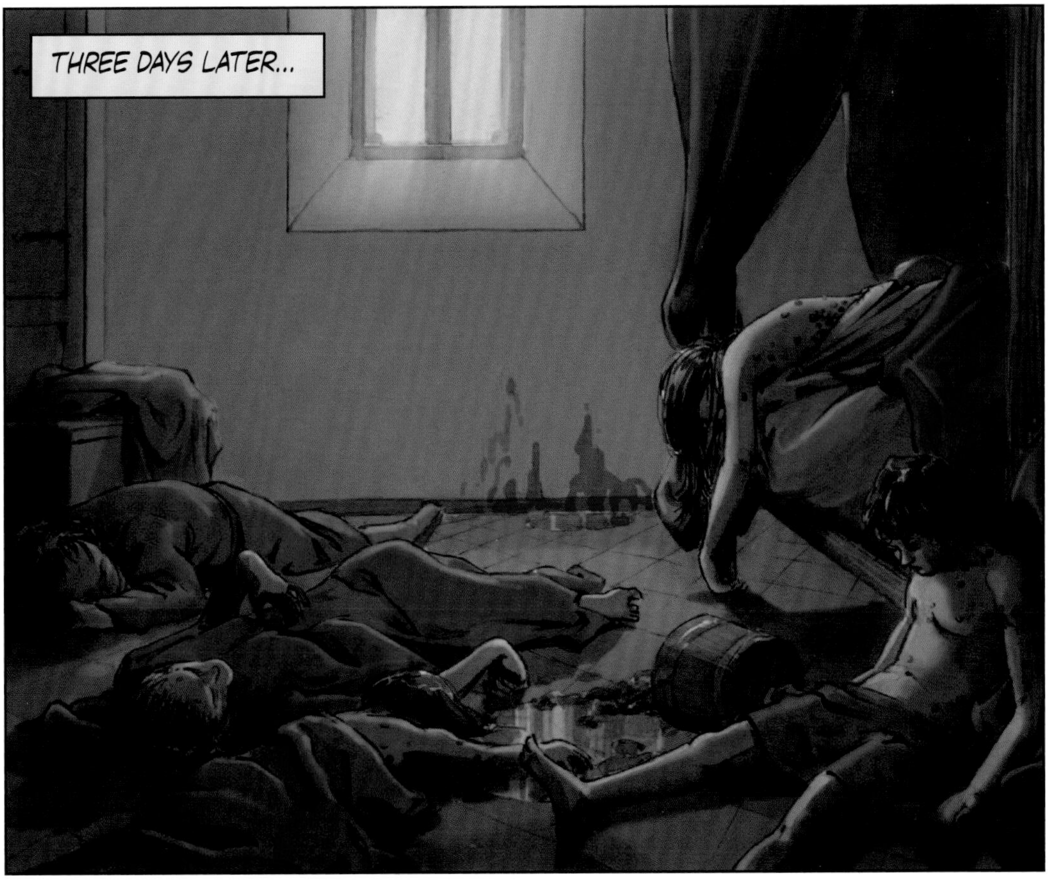
THREE DAYS LATER...

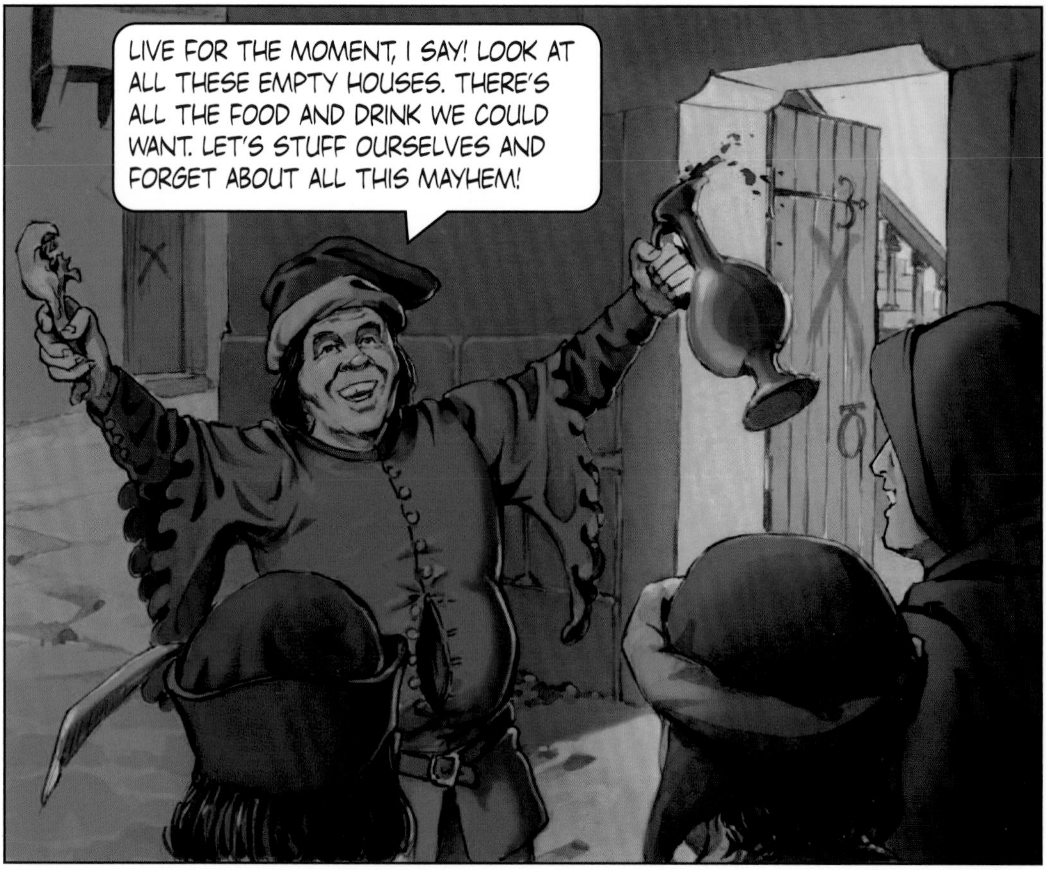
LIVE FOR THE MOMENT, I SAY! LOOK AT ALL THESE EMPTY HOUSES. THERE'S ALL THE FOOD AND DRINK WE COULD WANT. LET'S STUFF OURSELVES AND FORGET ABOUT ALL THIS MAYHEM!

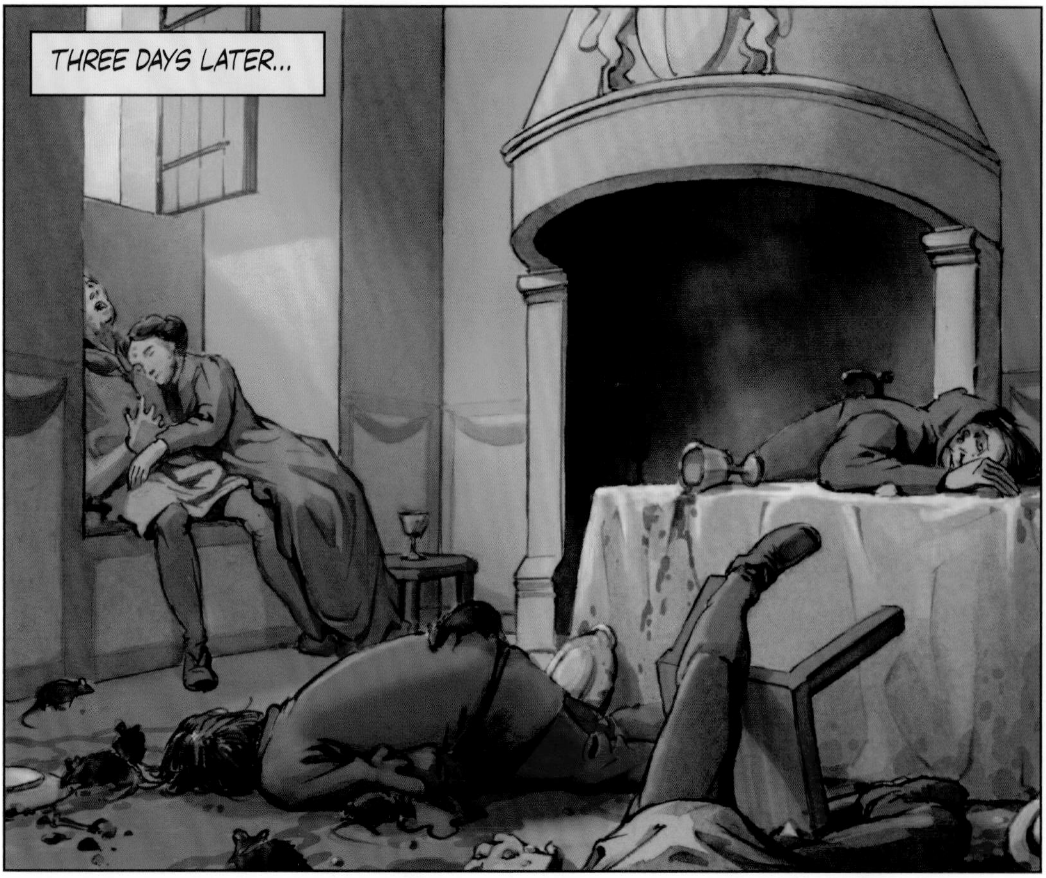
THREE DAYS LATER...

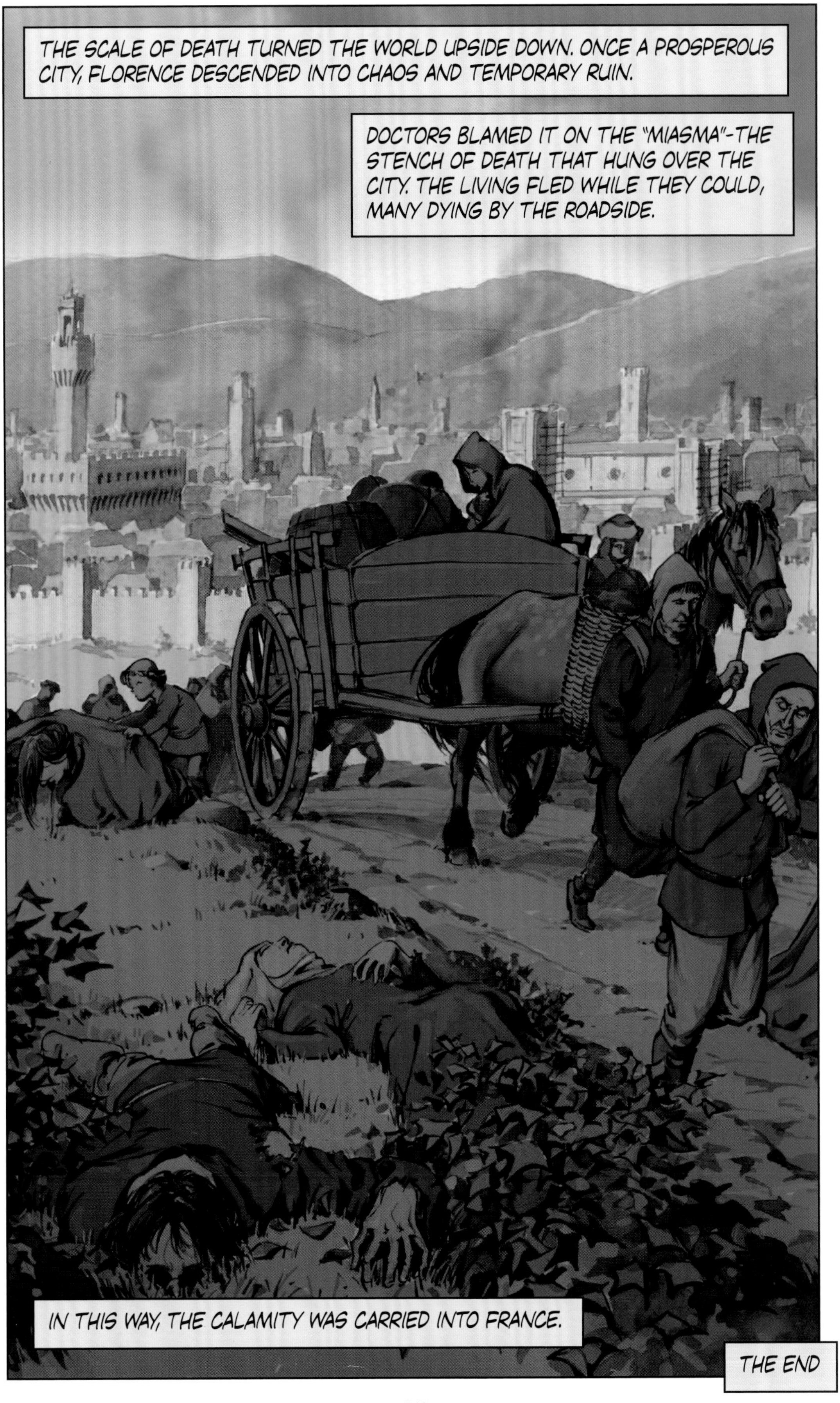
THE SCALE OF DEATH TURNED THE WORLD UPSIDE DOWN. ONCE A PROSPEROUS CITY, FLORENCE DESCENDED INTO CHAOS AND TEMPORARY RUIN.
DOCTORS BLAMED IT ON THE "MIASMA"-THE STENCH OF DEATH THAT HUNG OVER THE CITY. THE LIVING FLED WHILE THEY COULD, MANY DYING BY THE ROADSIDE.
IN THIS WAY, THE CALAMITY WAS CARRIED INTO FRANCE.
THE END

The Plague Reaches England

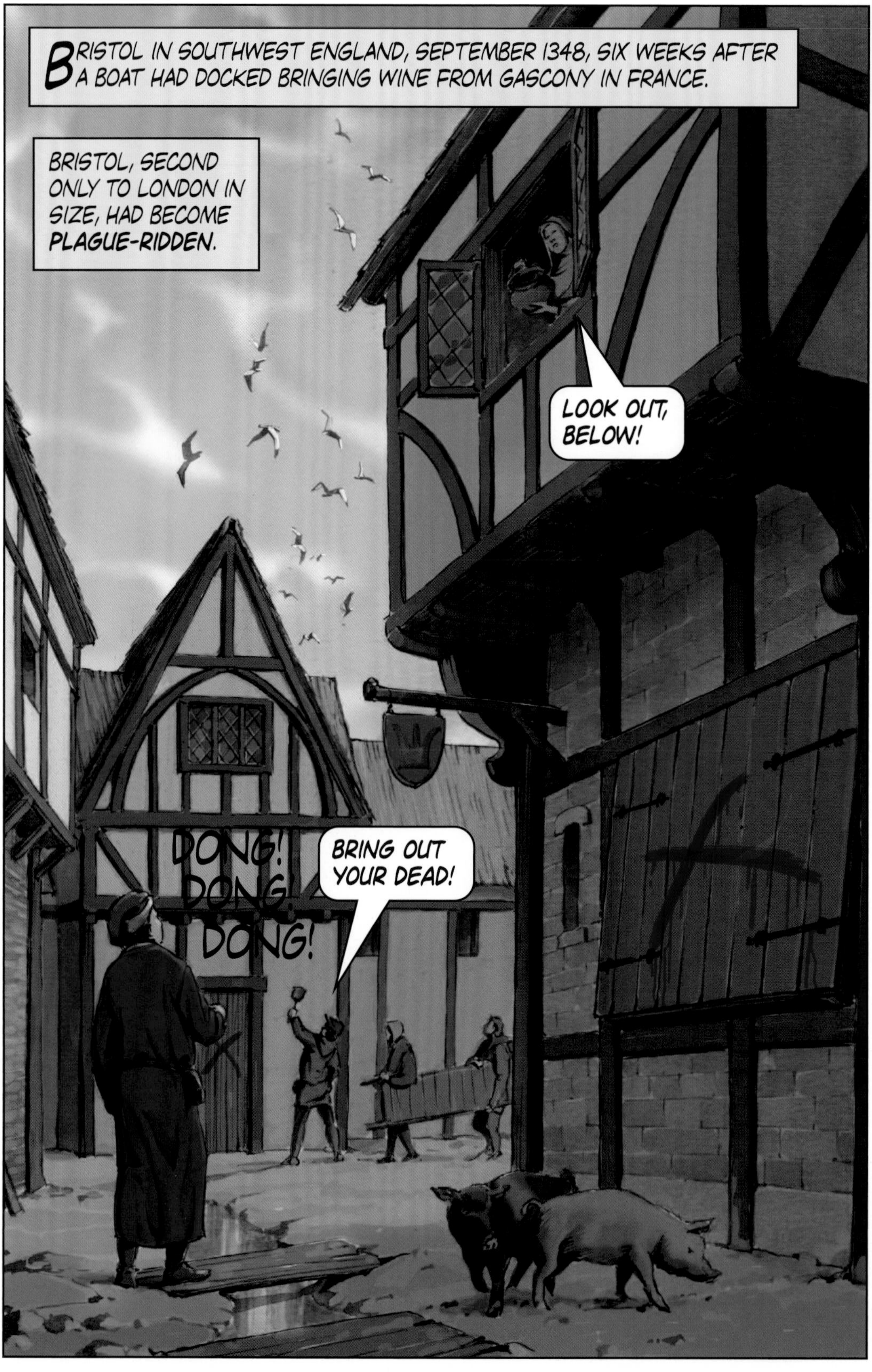

BRISTOL IN SOUTHWEST ENGLAND, SEPTEMBER 1348, SIX WEEKS AFTER A BOAT HAD DOCKED BRINGING WINE FROM GASCONY IN FRANCE.
BRISTOL, SECOND ONLY TO LONDON IN SIZE, HAD BECOME PLAGUE-RIDDEN.
LOOK OUT, BELOW!
DONG! DONG! DONG!
BRING OUT YOUR DEAD!

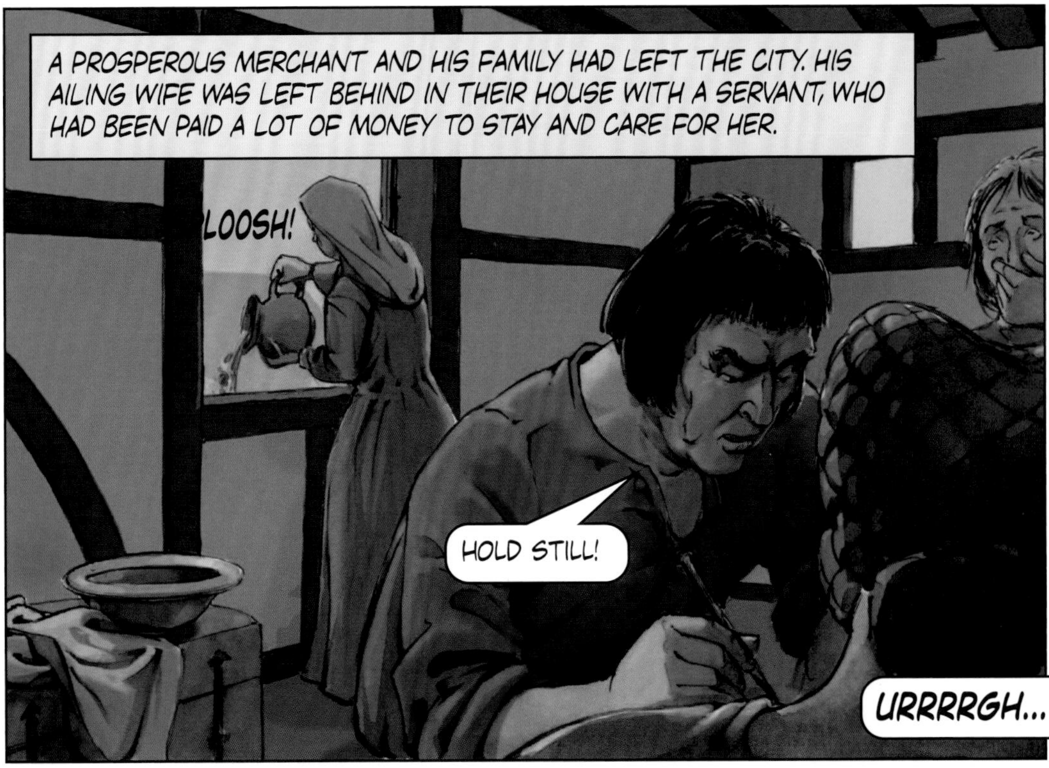
A PROSPEROUS MERCHANT AND HIS FAMILY HAD LEFT THE CITY. HIS AILING WIFE WAS LEFT BEHIND IN THEIR HOUSE WITH A SERVANT, WHO HAD BEEN PAID A LOT OF MONEY TO STAY AND CARE FOR HER.
LOOSH!
HOLD STILL!
URRRRGH...

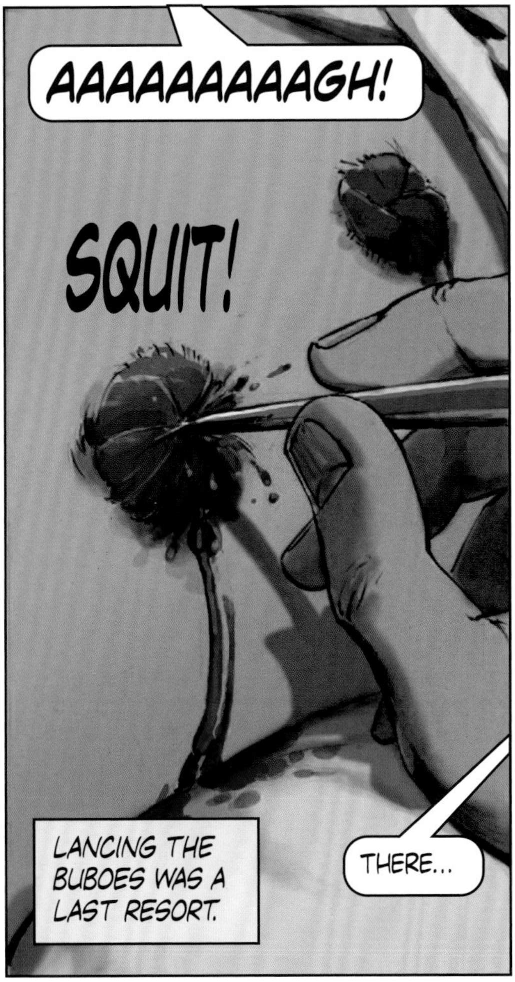
AAAAAAAAAGH!
SQUIT!
LANCING THE BUBOES WAS A LAST RESORT.
THERE...

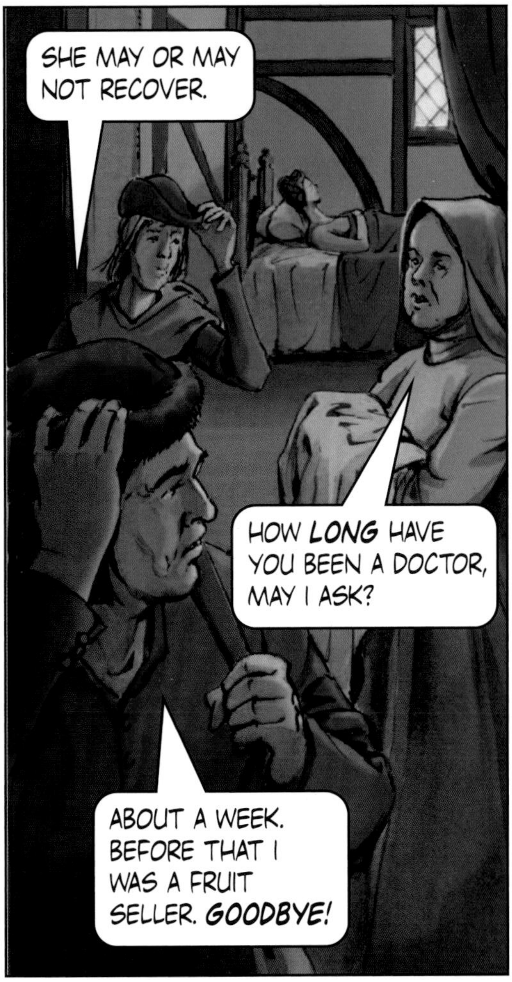
SHE MAY OR MAY NOT RECOVER.
HOW LONG HAVE YOU BEEN A DOCTOR, MAY I ASK?
ABOUT A WEEK. BEFORE THAT I WAS A FRUIT SELLER. GOODBYE!

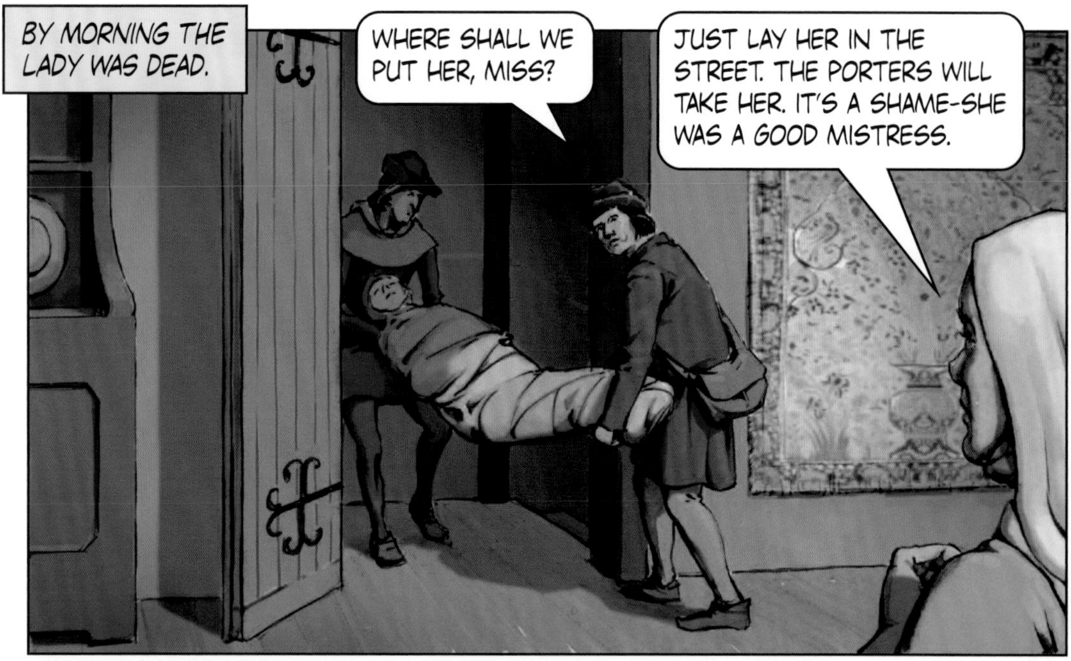
BY MORNING THE LADY WAS DEAD.
WHERE SHALL WE PUT HER, MISS?
JUST LAY HER IN THE STREET. THE PORTERS WILL TAKE HER. IT'S A SHAME-SHE WAS A GOOD MISTRESS.

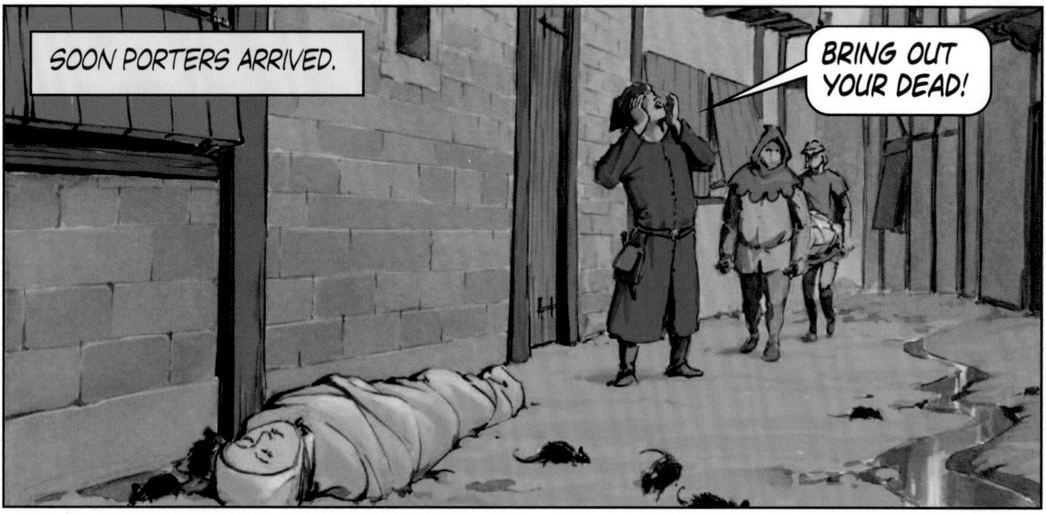
SOON PORTERS ARRIVED.
BRING OUT YOUR DEAD!

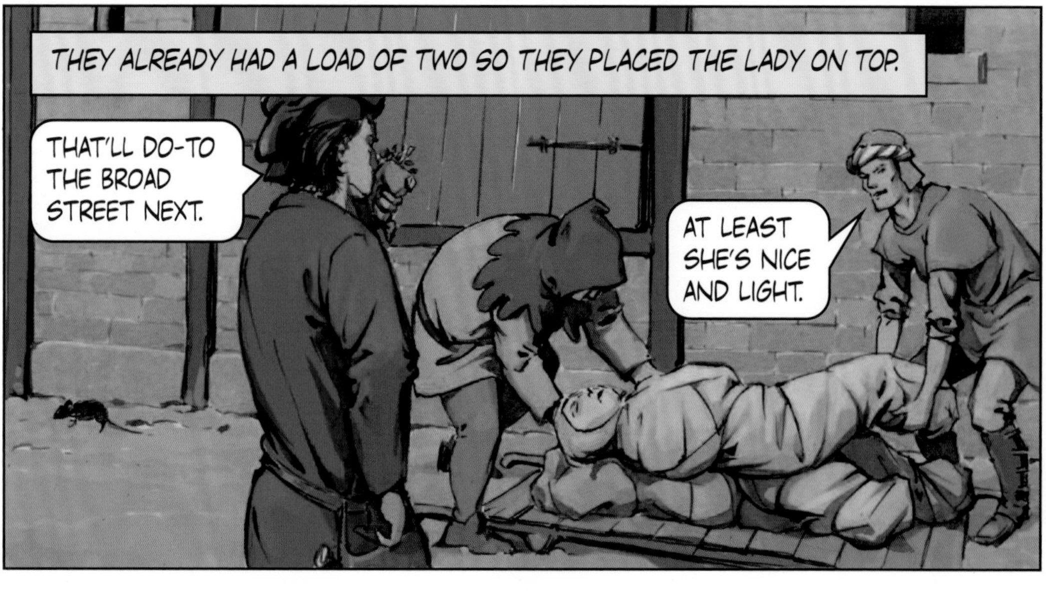
THEY ALREADY HAD A LOAD OF TWO SO THEY PLACED THE LADY ON TOP.
THAT'LL DO-TO THE BROAD STREET NEXT.
AT LEAST SHE'S NICE AND LIGHT.

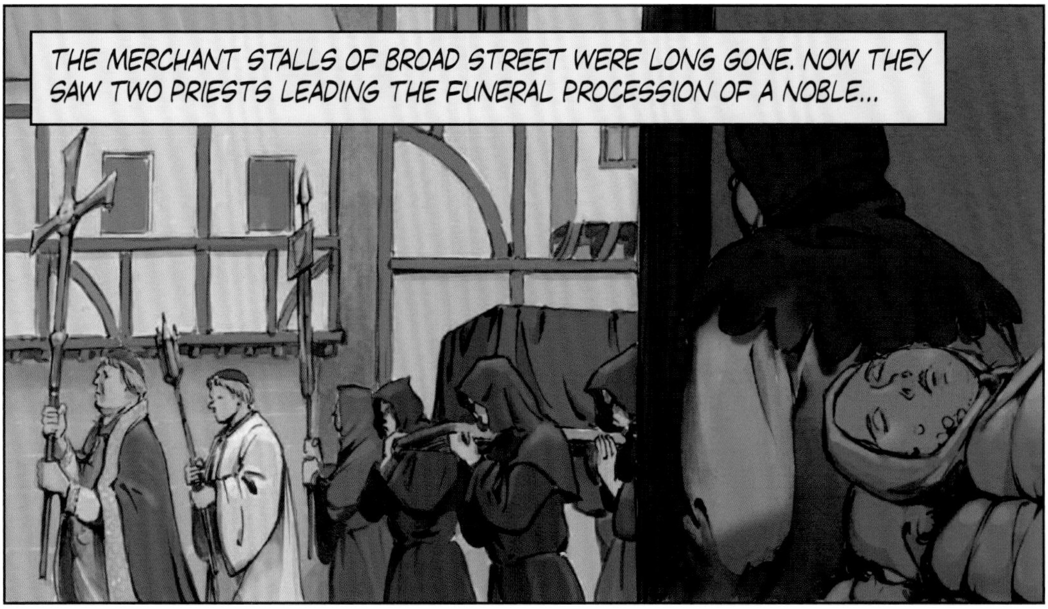
THE MERCHANT STALLS OF BROAD STREET WERE LONG GONE. NOW THEY SAW TWO PRIESTS LEADING THE FUNERAL PROCESSION OF A NOBLE...

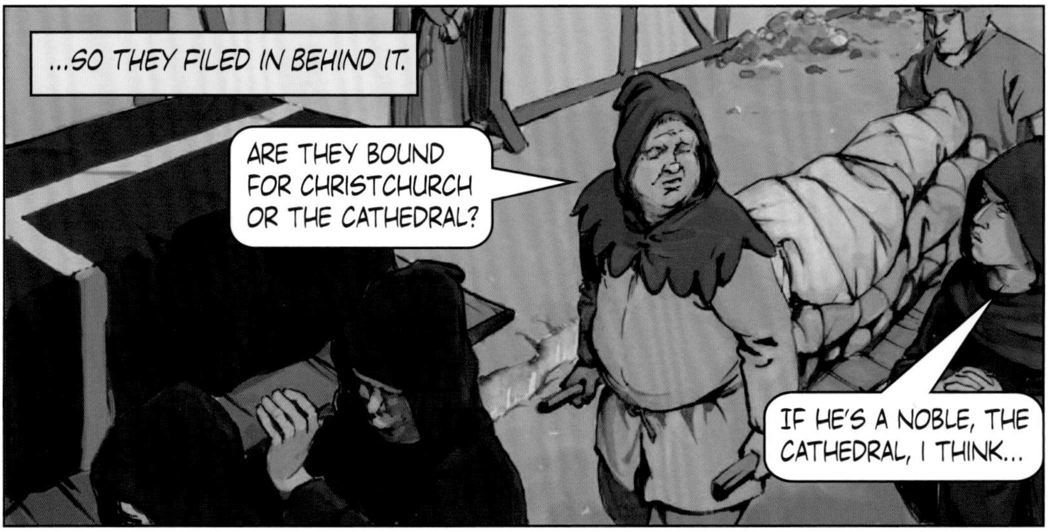
...SO THEY FILED IN BEHIND IT.
ARE THEY BOUND FOR CHRISTCHURCH OR THE CATHEDRAL?
IF HE'S A NOBLE, THE CATHEDRAL, I THINK...

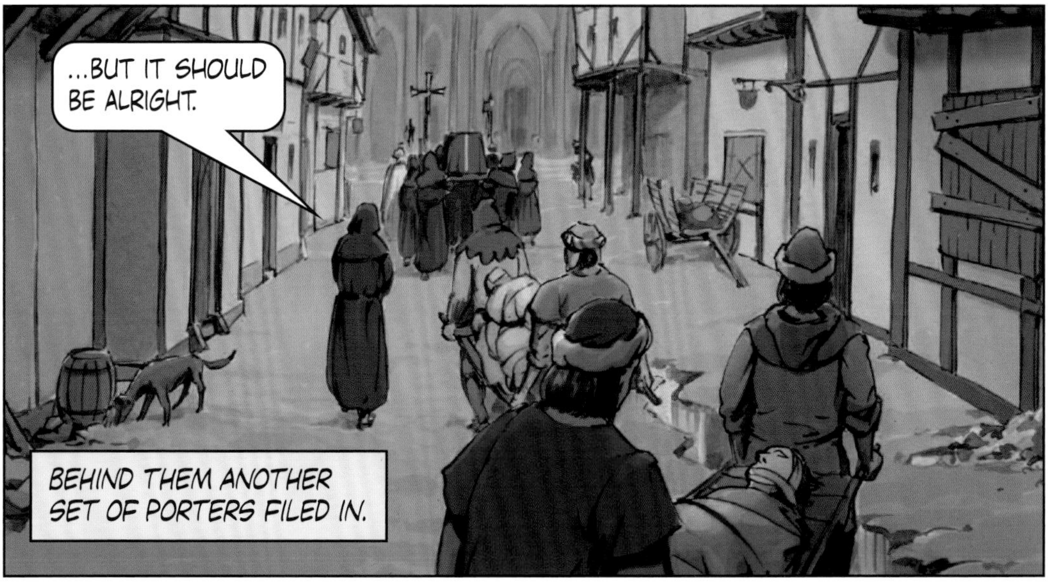
...BUT IT SHOULD BE ALRIGHT.
BEHIND THEM ANOTHER SET OF PORTERS FILED IN.

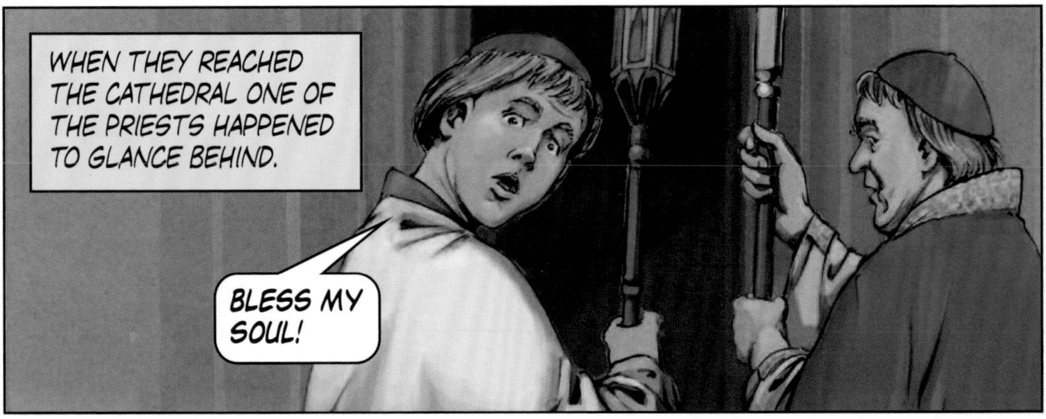
WHEN THEY REACHED THE CATHEDRAL ONE OF THE PRIESTS HAPPENED TO GLANCE BEHIND.
BLESS MY SOUL!

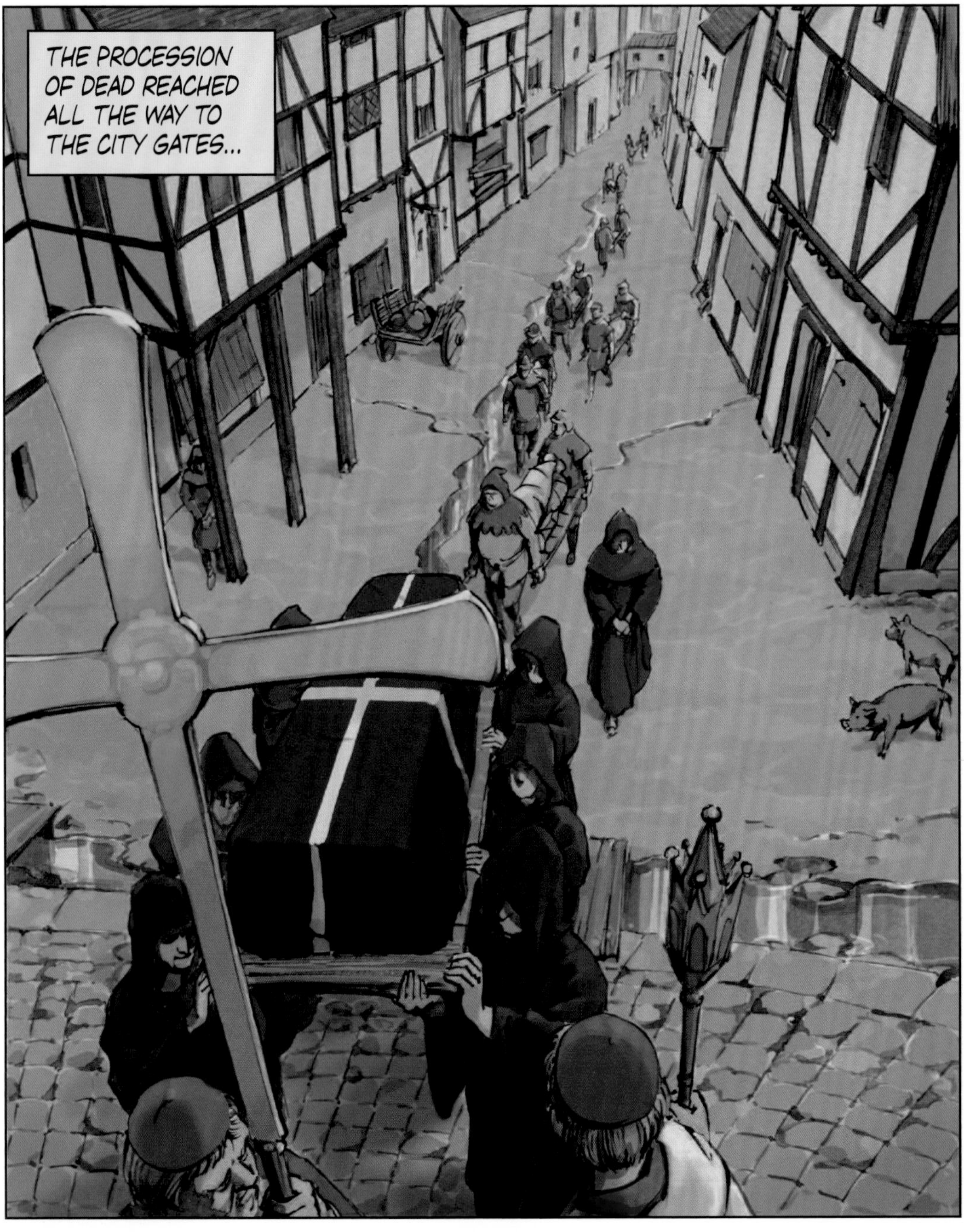
THE PROCESSION OF DEAD REACHED ALL THE WAY TO THE CITY GATES...

AFTER THE NOBLE'S BURIAL...

WE WILL SOON BE OUT OF HOLY GROUND TO BURY THE PEOPLE OF BRISTOL.

SO WHAT CAN WE DO? WHERE WILL WE PUT THEM?

AND WHAT HAPPENS IF WE GO, TOO? WHO WILL BE HERE TO MINISTER TO THE SICK?

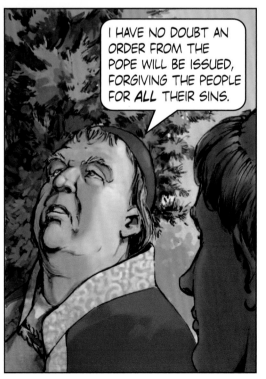

I HAVE NO DOUBT AN ORDER FROM THE POPE WILL BE ISSUED, FORGIVING THE PEOPLE FOR **ALL** THEIR SINS.

IT WOULD BE FITTING IN THIS TIME OF...**CRISIS.**

WHAT'S HAPPENING, YOUR GRACE? IS THE WORLD ENDING?

The Plague in London

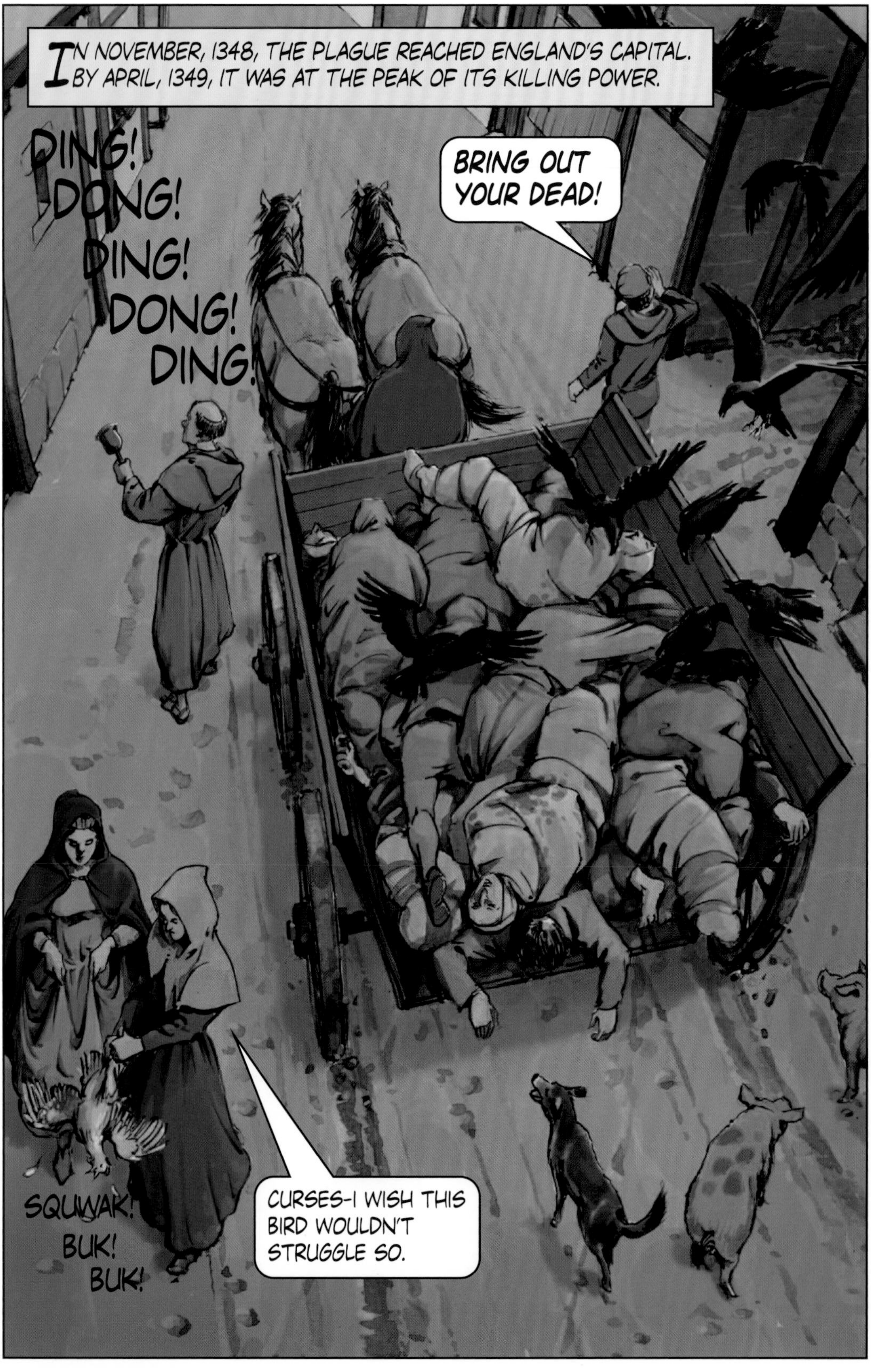
IN NOVEMBER, 1348, THE PLAGUE REACHED ENGLAND'S CAPITAL. BY APRIL, 1349, IT WAS AT THE PEAK OF ITS KILLING POWER.
DING! DONG! DING! DONG! DING!
BRING OUT YOUR DEAD!
SQUWAK! BUK! BUK!
CURSES-I WISH THIS BIRD WOULDN'T STRUGGLE SO.

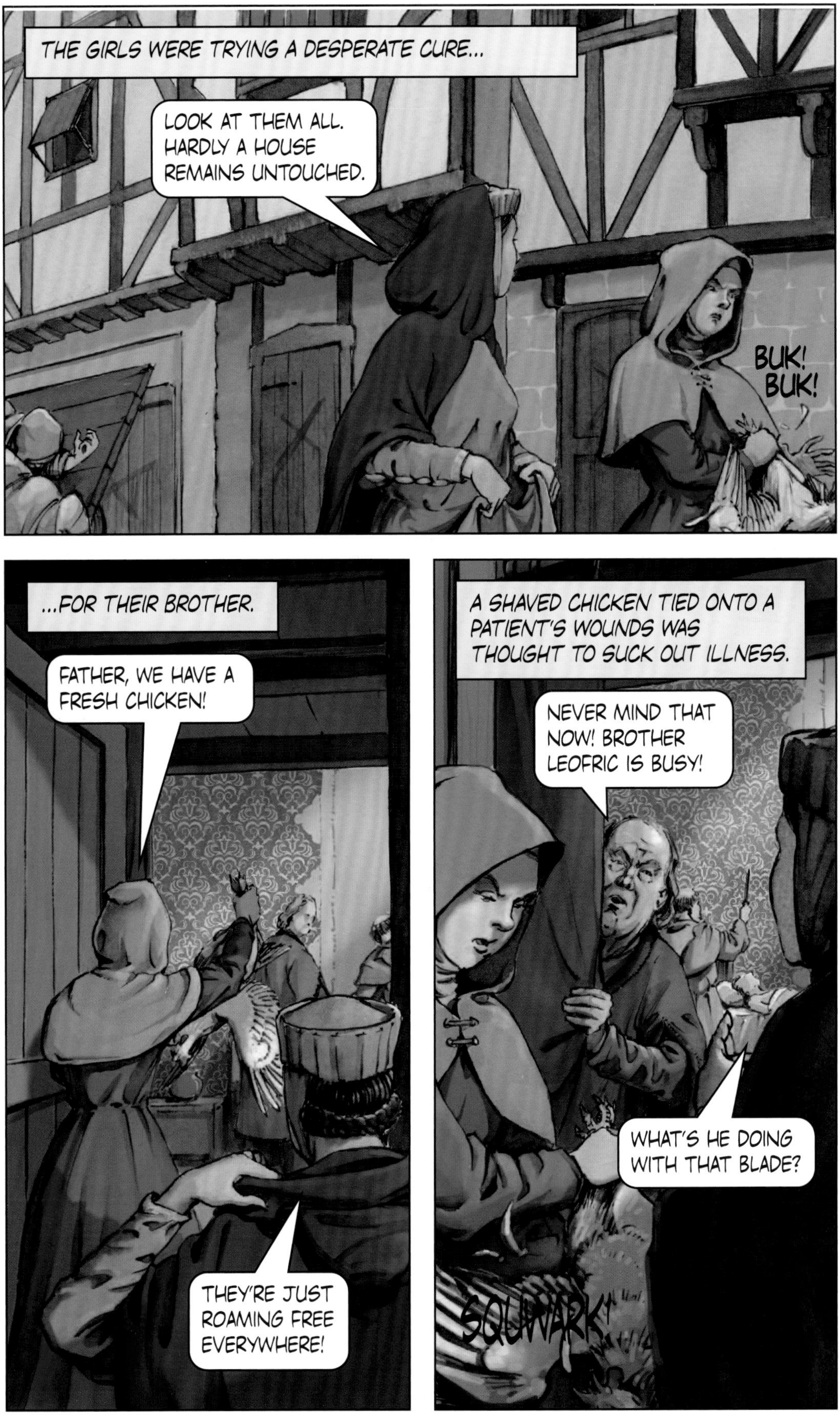
THE GIRLS WERE TRYING A DESPERATE CURE...
LOOK AT THEM ALL. HARDLY A HOUSE REMAINS UNTOUCHED.
BUK! BUK!
...FOR THEIR BROTHER.
FATHER, WE HAVE A FRESH CHICKEN!
THEY'RE JUST ROAMING FREE EVERYWHERE!
A SHAVED CHICKEN TIED ONTO A PATIENT'S WOUNDS WAS THOUGHT TO SUCK OUT ILLNESS.
NEVER MIND THAT NOW! BROTHER LEOFRIC IS BUSY!
WHAT'S HE DOING WITH THAT BLADE?
SQUWARK!

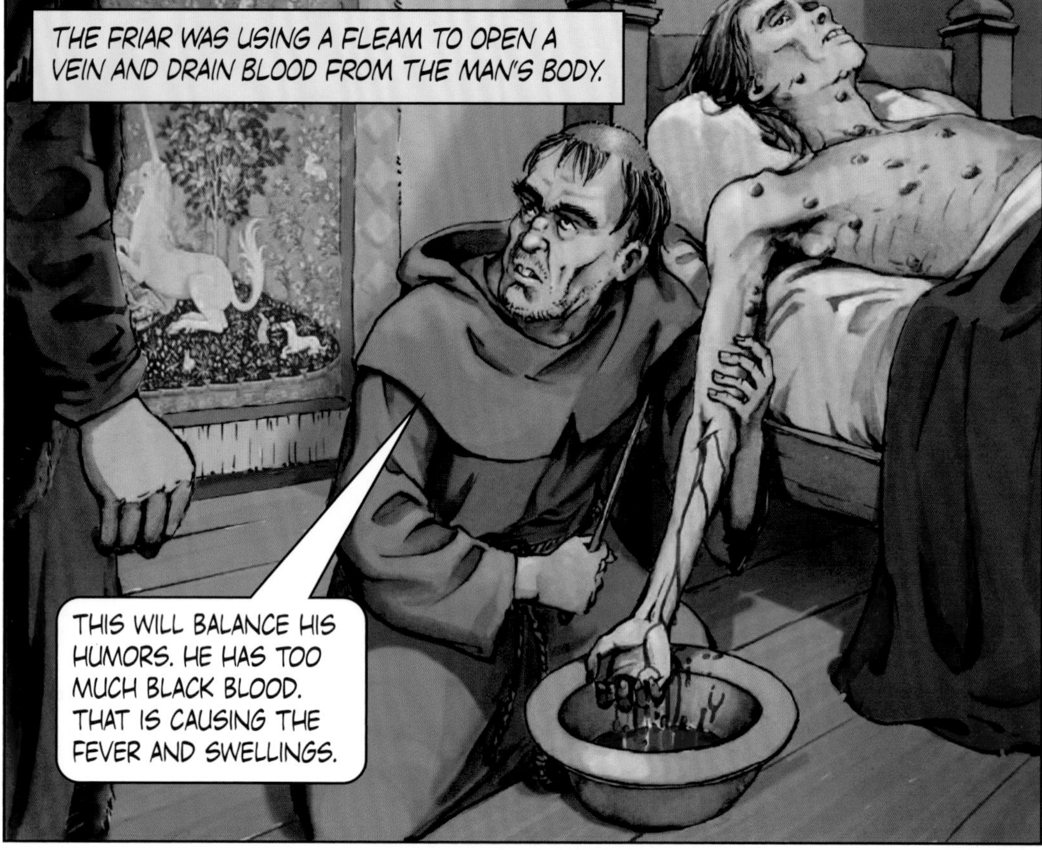
THE FRIAR WAS USING A FLEAM TO OPEN A VEIN AND DRAIN BLOOD FROM THE MAN'S BODY.
THIS WILL BALANCE HIS HUMORS. HE HAS TOO MUCH BLACK BLOOD. THAT IS CAUSING THE FEVER AND SWELLINGS.

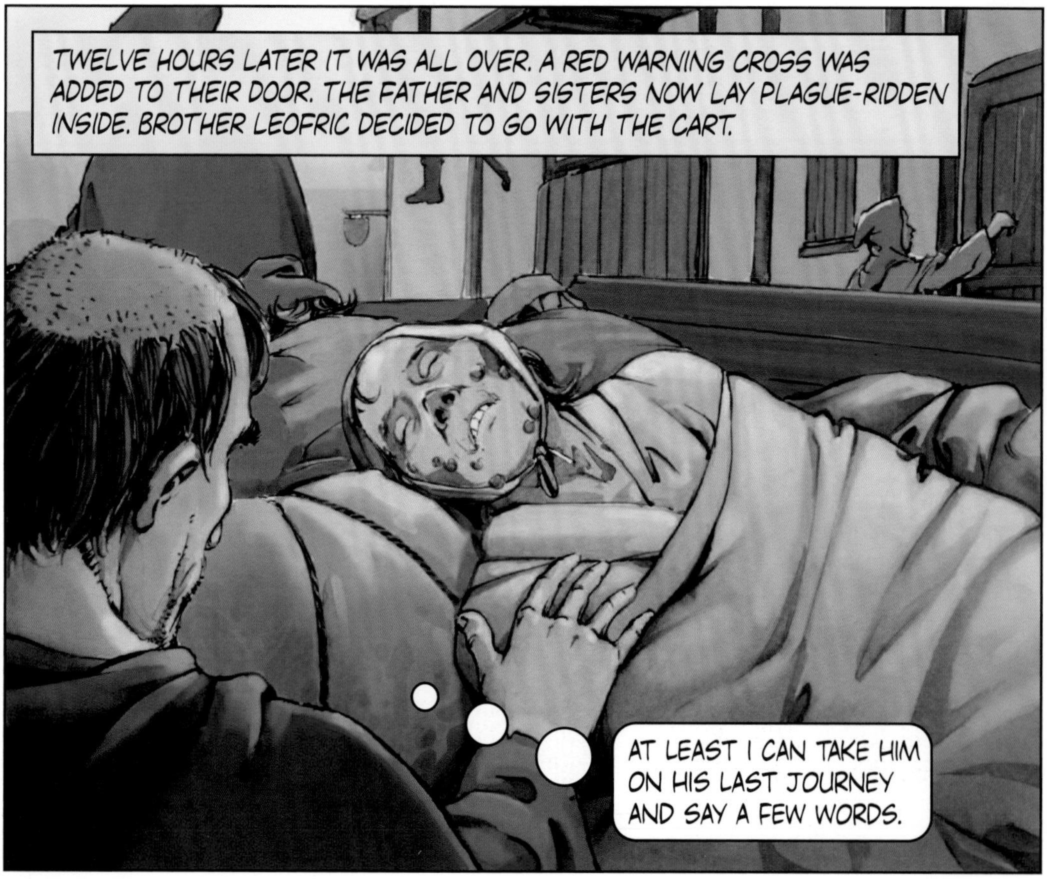
TWELVE HOURS LATER IT WAS ALL OVER. A RED WARNING CROSS WAS ADDED TO THEIR DOOR. THE FATHER AND SISTERS NOW LAY PLAGUE-RIDDEN INSIDE. BROTHER LEOFRIC DECIDED TO GO WITH THE CART.
AT LEAST I CAN TAKE HIM ON HIS LAST JOURNEY AND SAY A FEW WORDS.

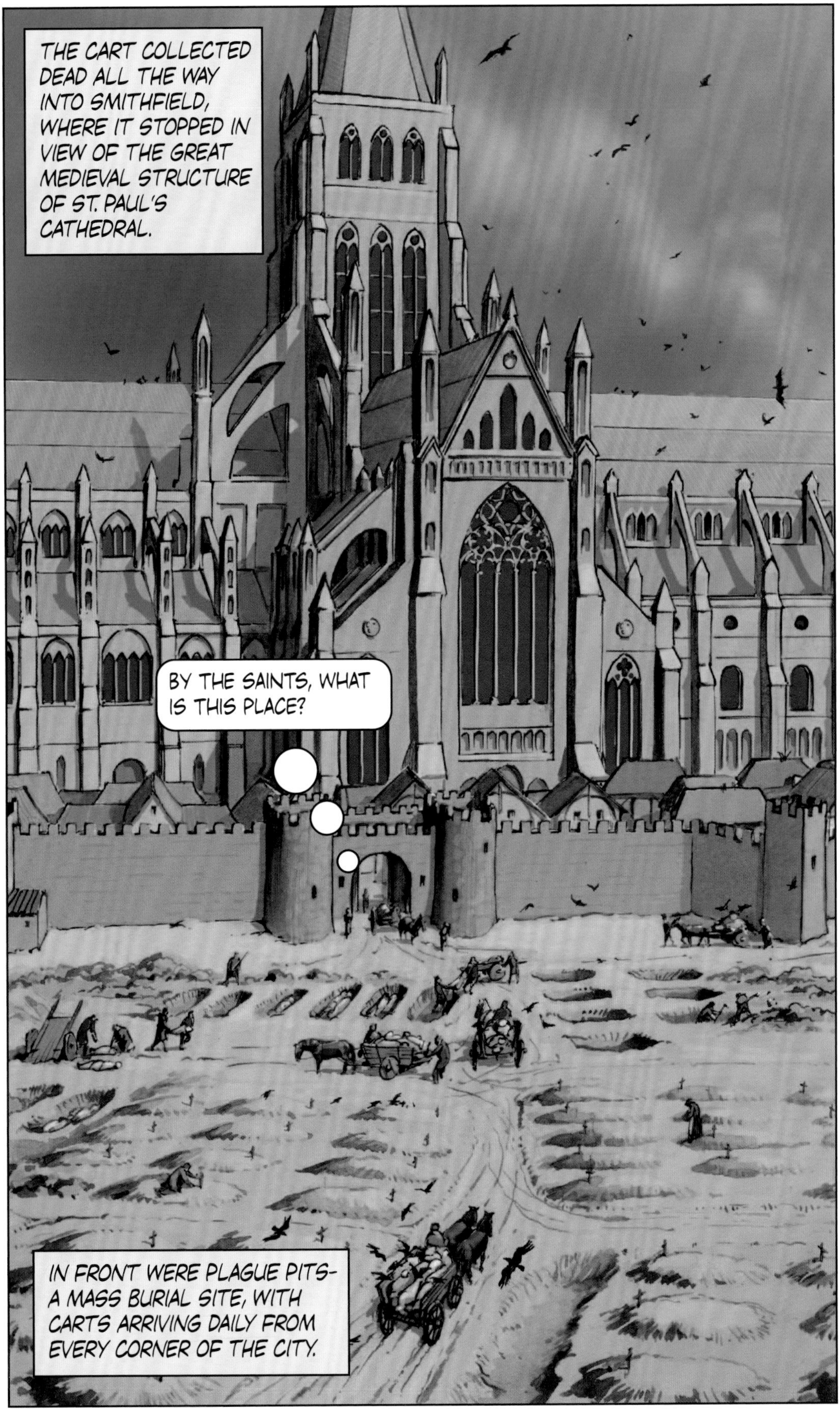
THE CART COLLECTED DEAD ALL THE WAY INTO SMITHFIELD, WHERE IT STOPPED IN VIEW OF THE GREAT MEDIEVAL STRUCTURE OF ST. PAUL'S CATHEDRAL.
BY THE SAINTS, WHAT IS THIS PLACE?
IN FRONT WERE PLAGUE PITS- A MASS BURIAL SITE, WITH CARTS ARRIVING DAILY FROM EVERY CORNER OF THE CITY.

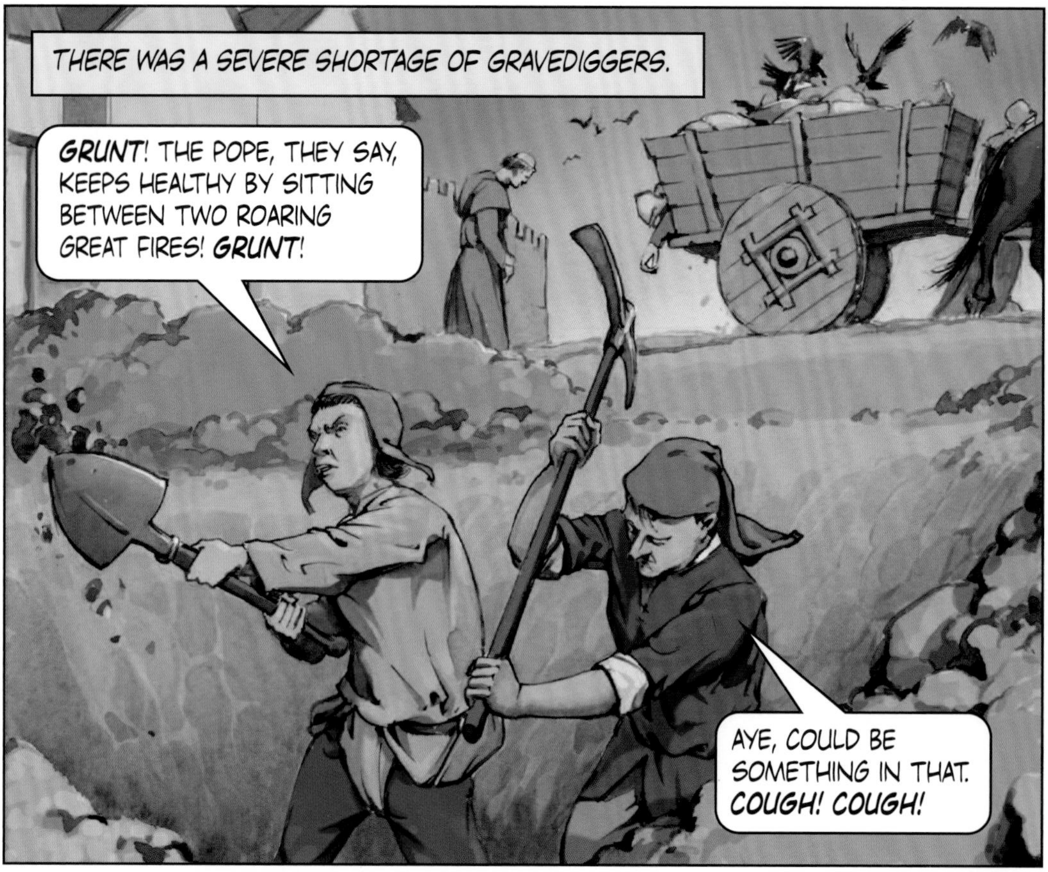
THERE WAS A SEVERE SHORTAGE OF GRAVEDIGGERS.
GRUNT! THE POPE, THEY SAY, KEEPS HEALTHY BY SITTING BETWEEN TWO ROARING GREAT FIRES! GRUNT!
AYE, COULD BE SOMETHING IN THAT. COUGH! COUGH!

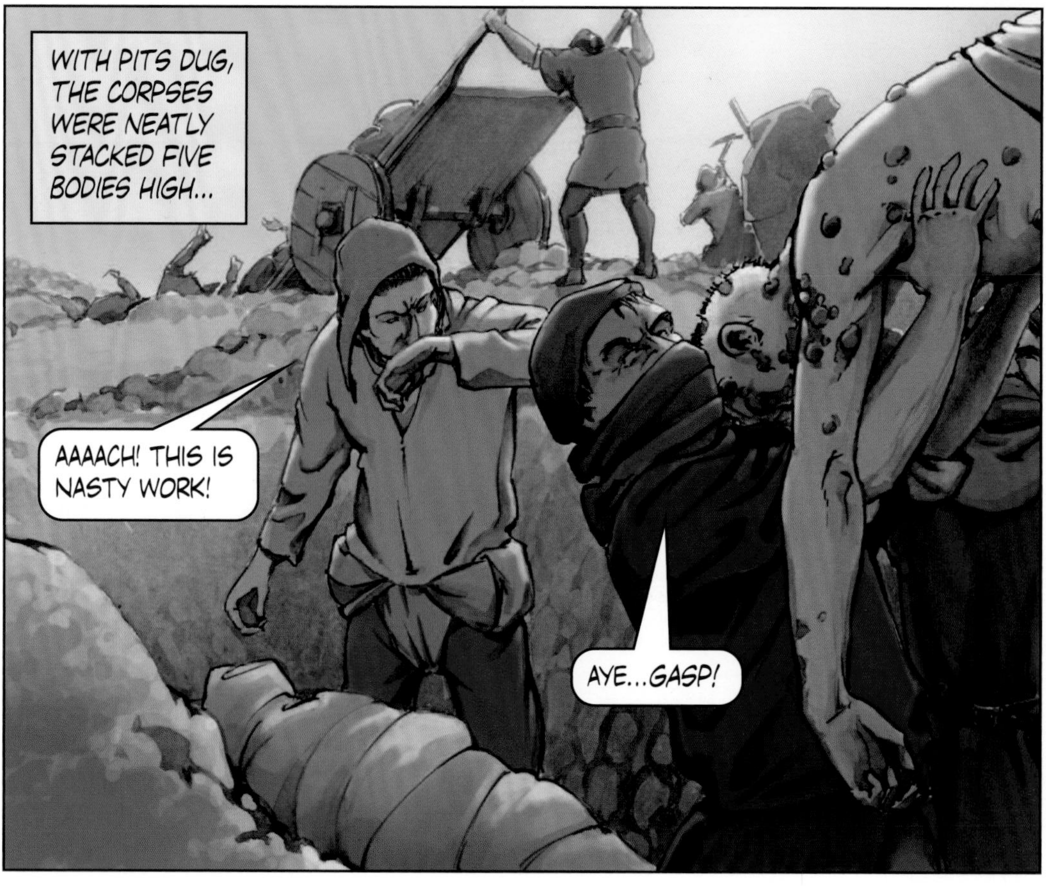
WITH PITS DUG, THE CORPSES WERE NEATLY STACKED FIVE BODIES HIGH...
AAAACH! THIS IS NASTY WORK!
AYE...GASP!

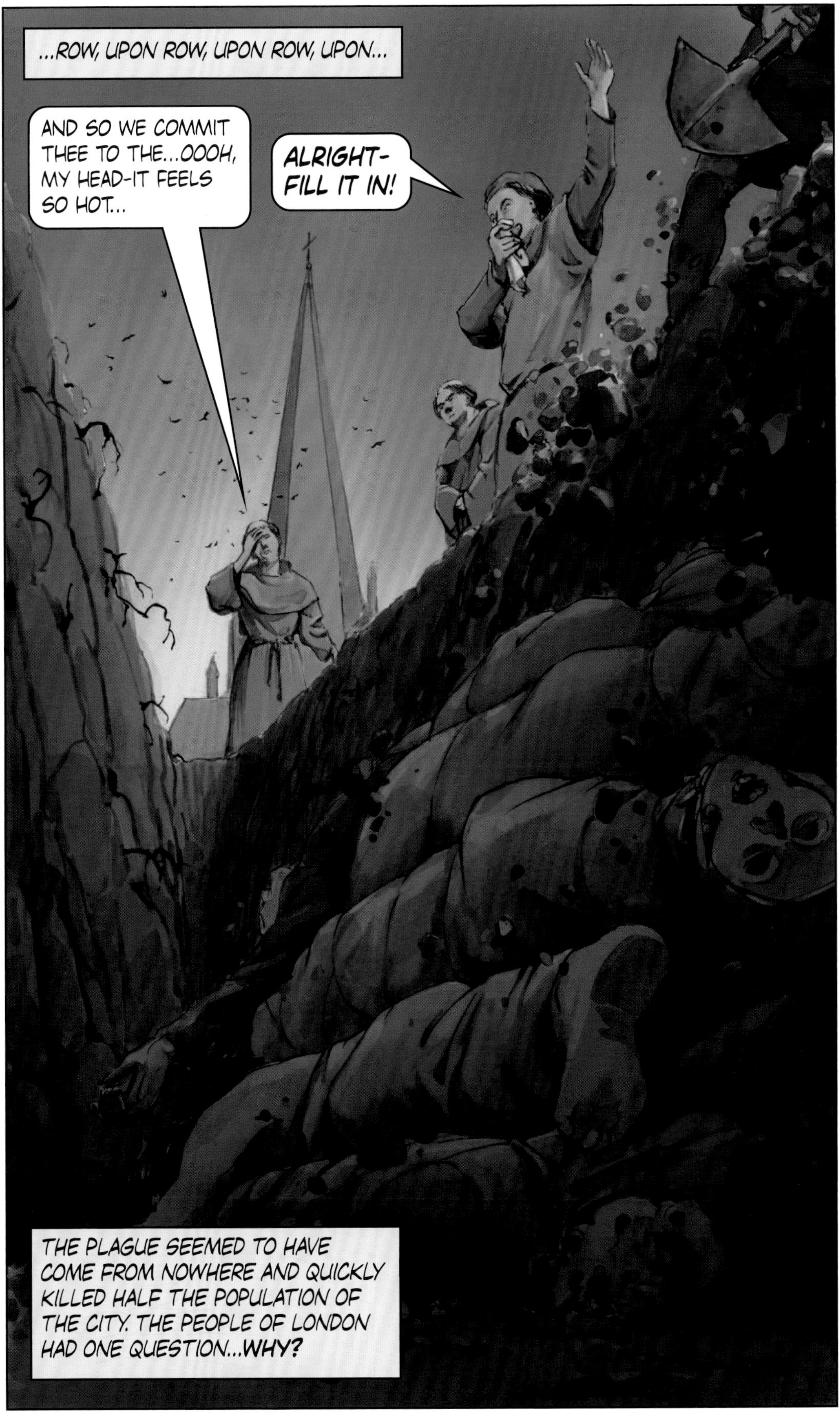

...ROW, UPON ROW, UPON ROW, UPON...
AND SO WE COMMIT THEE TO THE...OOOH, MY HEAD-IT FEELS SO HOT...
ALRIGHT-FILL IT IN!
THE PLAGUE SEEMED TO HAVE COME FROM NOWHERE AND QUICKLY KILLED HALF THE POPULATION OF THE CITY. THE PEOPLE OF LONDON HAD ONE QUESTION...WHY?

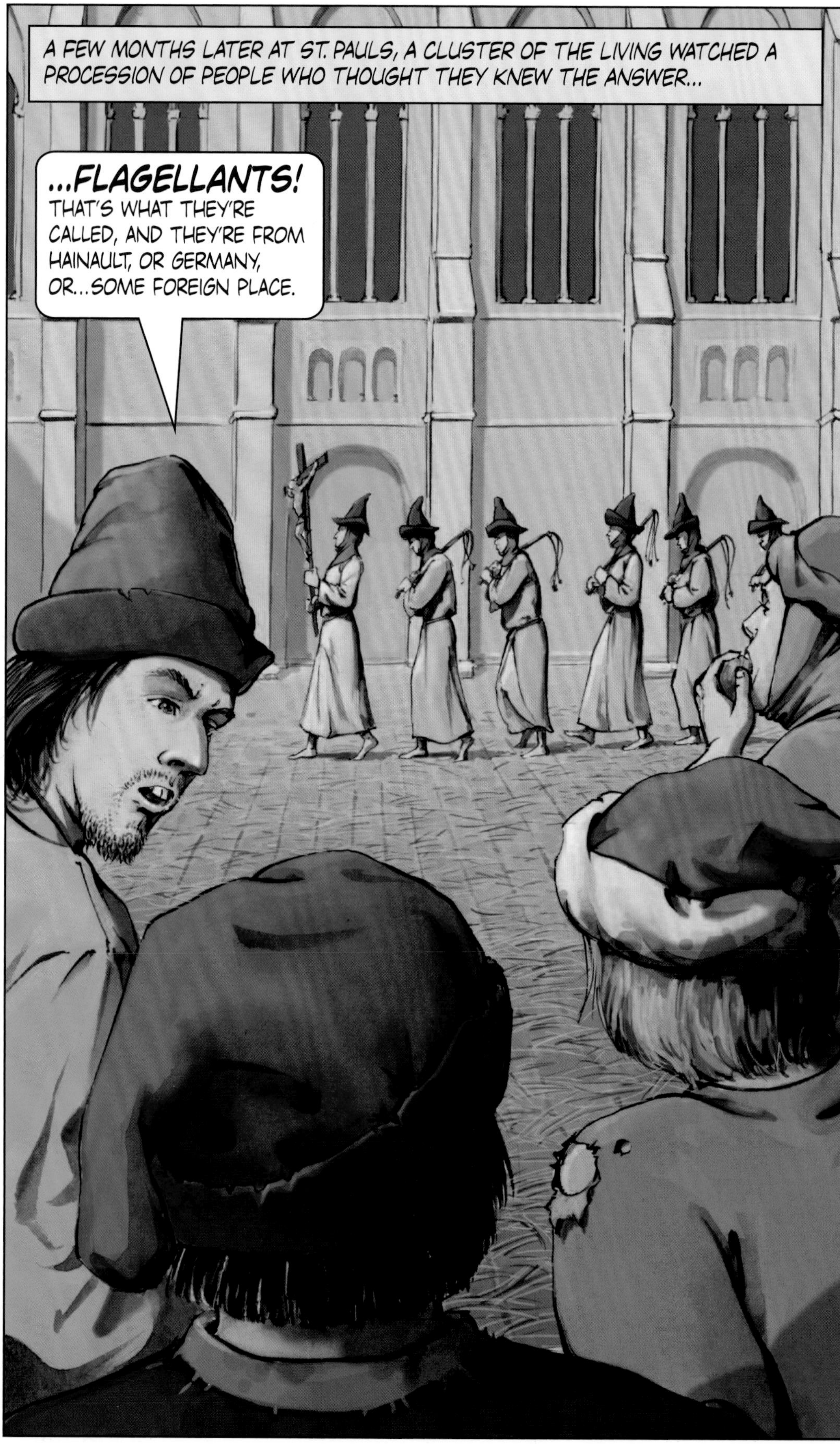
A FEW MONTHS LATER AT ST. PAULS, A CLUSTER OF THE LIVING WATCHED A PROCESSION OF PEOPLE WHO THOUGHT THEY KNEW THE ANSWER...
...FLAGELLANTS! THAT'S WHAT THEY'RE CALLED, AND THEY'RE FROM HAINAULT, OR GERMANY, OR...SOME FOREIGN PLACE.

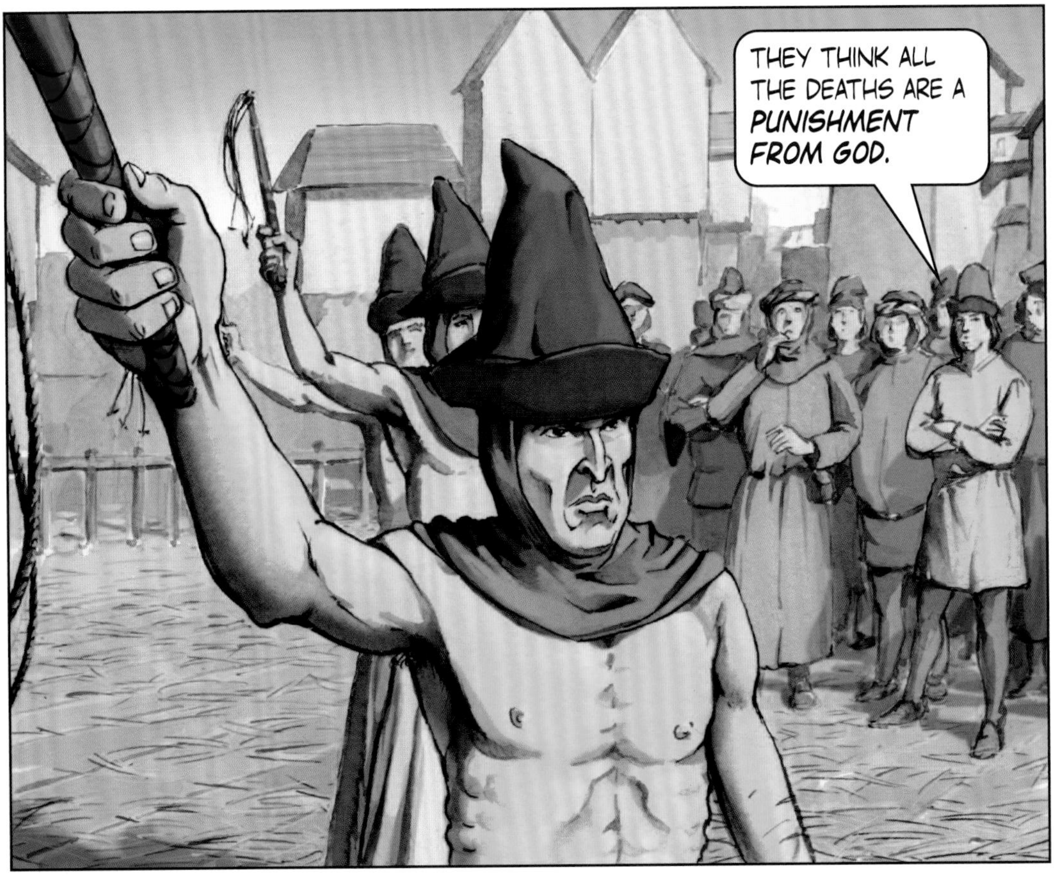
THEY THINK ALL THE DEATHS ARE A PUNISHMENT FROM GOD.

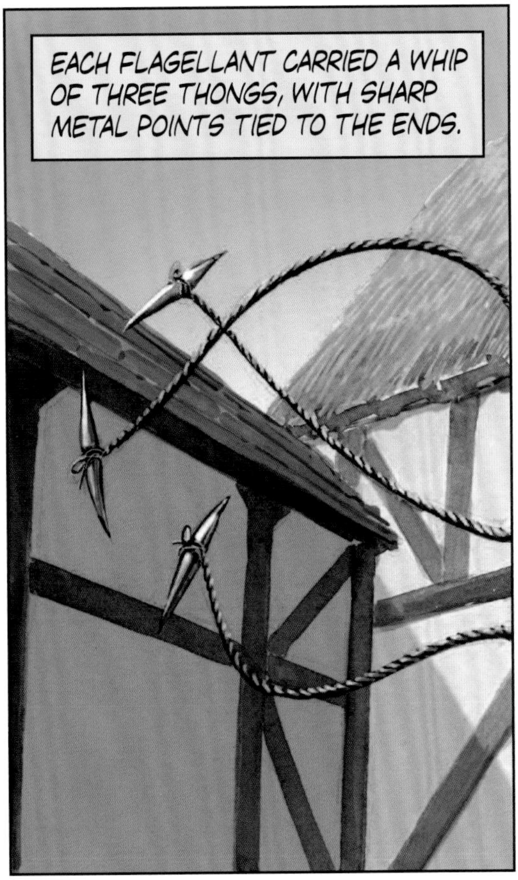
EACH FLAGELLANT CARRIED A WHIP OF THREE THONGS, WITH SHARP METAL POINTS TIED TO THE ENDS.

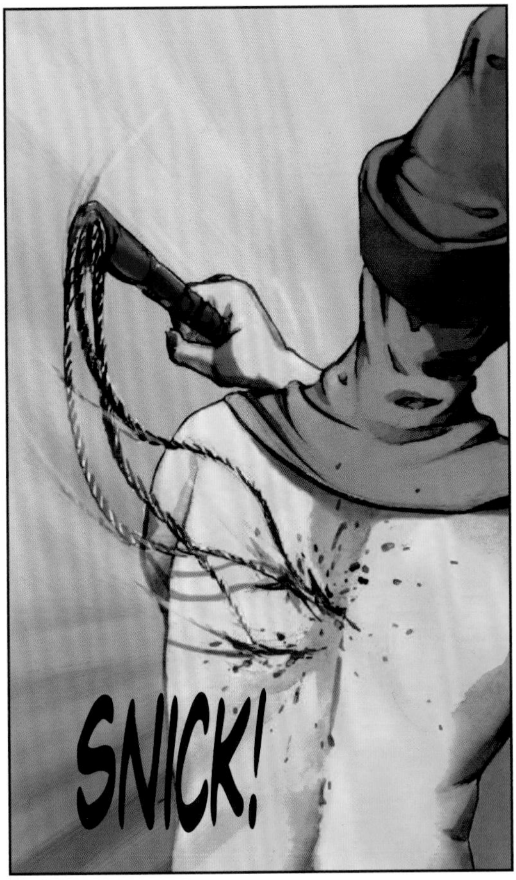
SNICK!

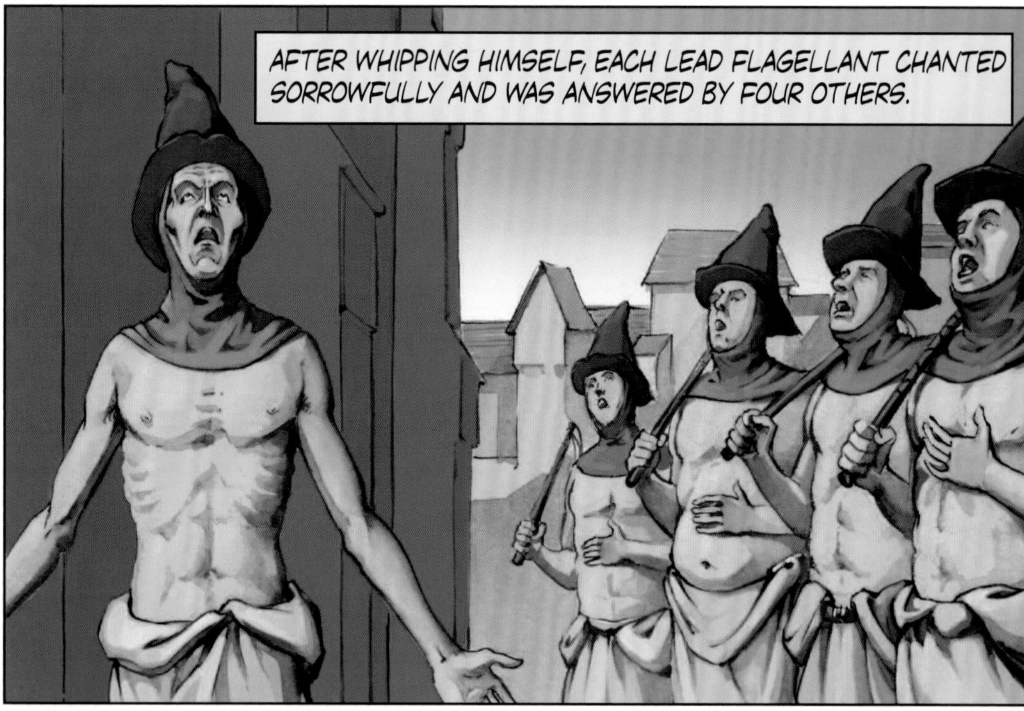
AFTER WHIPPING HIMSELF, EACH LEAD FLAGELLANT CHANTED SORROWFULLY AND WAS ANSWERED BY FOUR OTHERS.

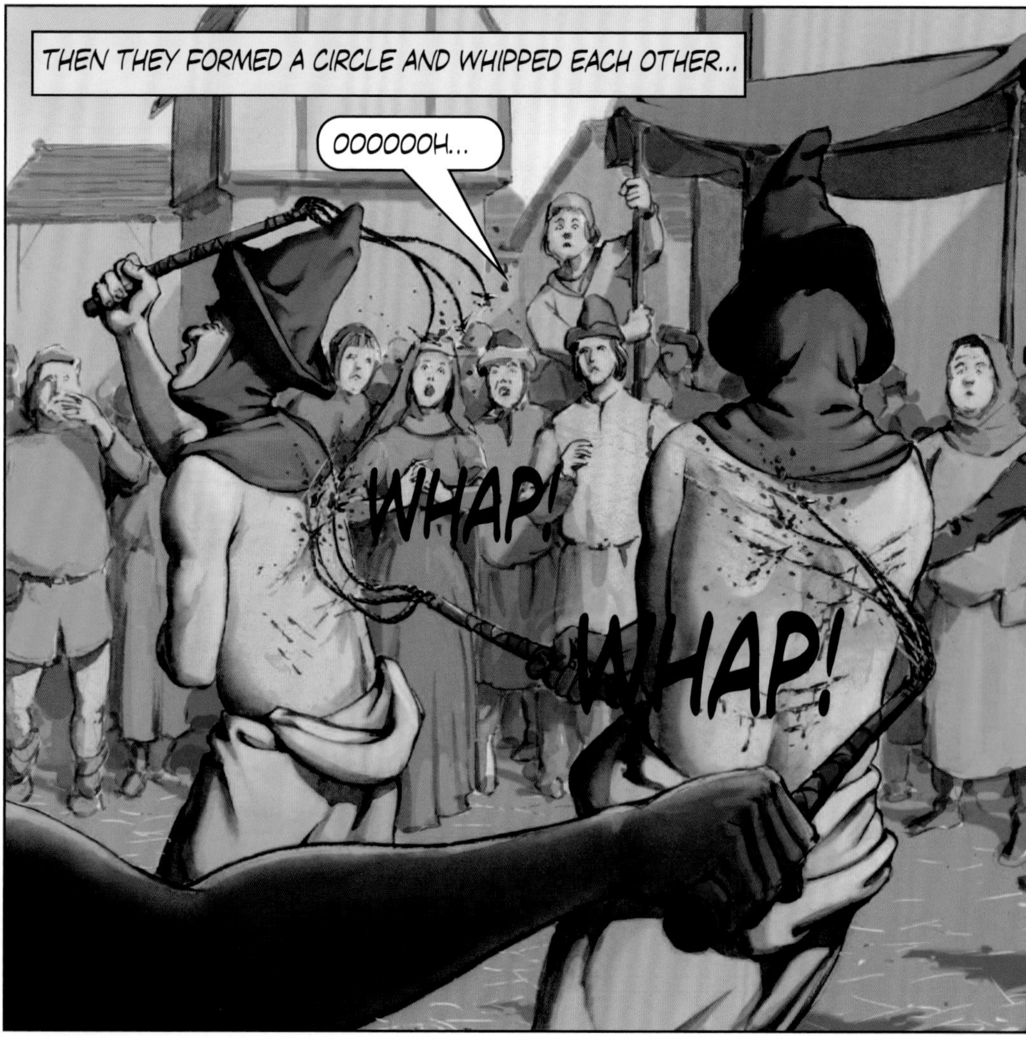
THEN THEY FORMED A CIRCLE AND WHIPPED EACH OTHER...
OOOOOOH...
WHAP!
WHAP!

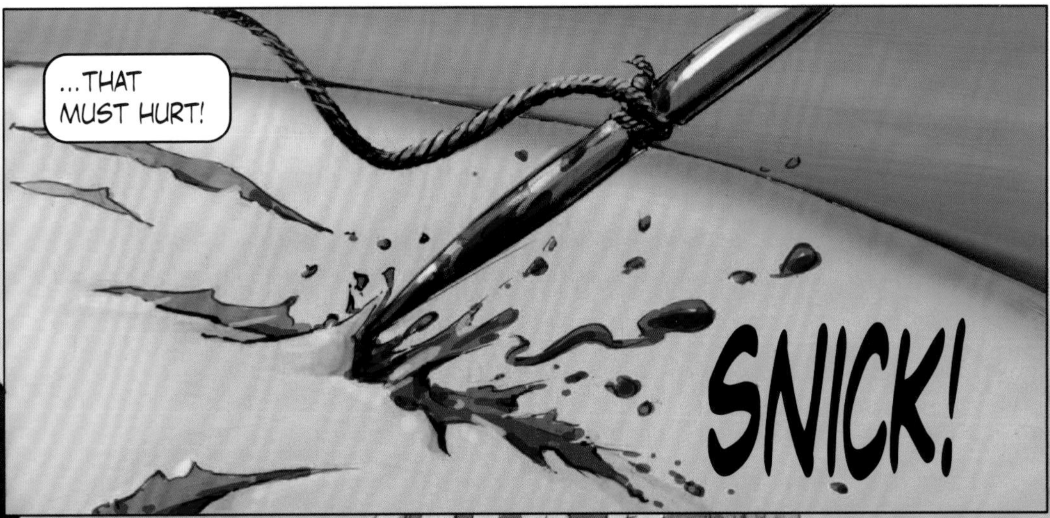
...THAT MUST HURT!
SNICK!

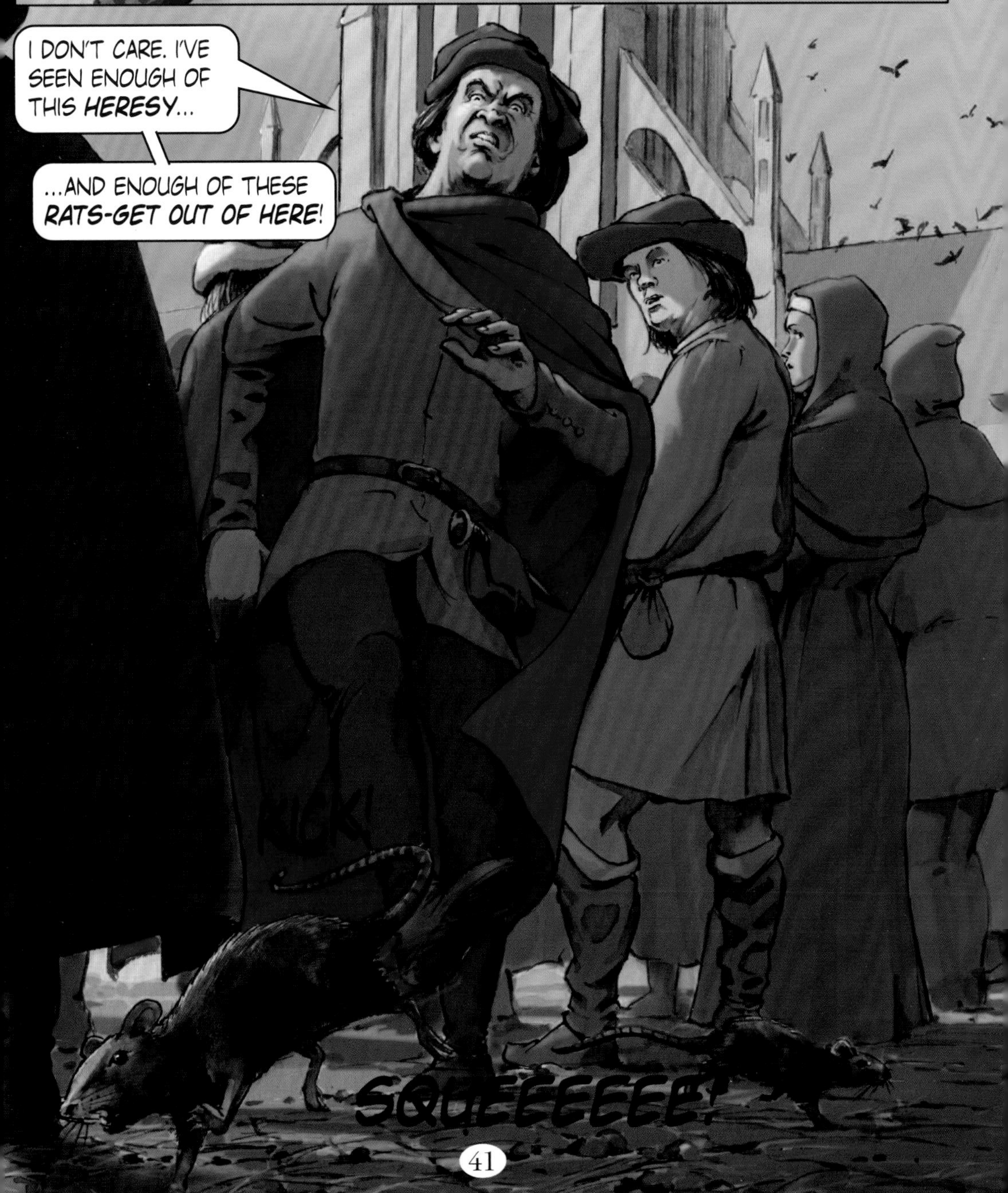
I DON'T CARE. I'VE SEEN ENOUGH OF THIS **HERESY**...
...AND ENOUGH OF THESE **RATS-GET OUT OF HERE!**
SQUEEEEEEEE!

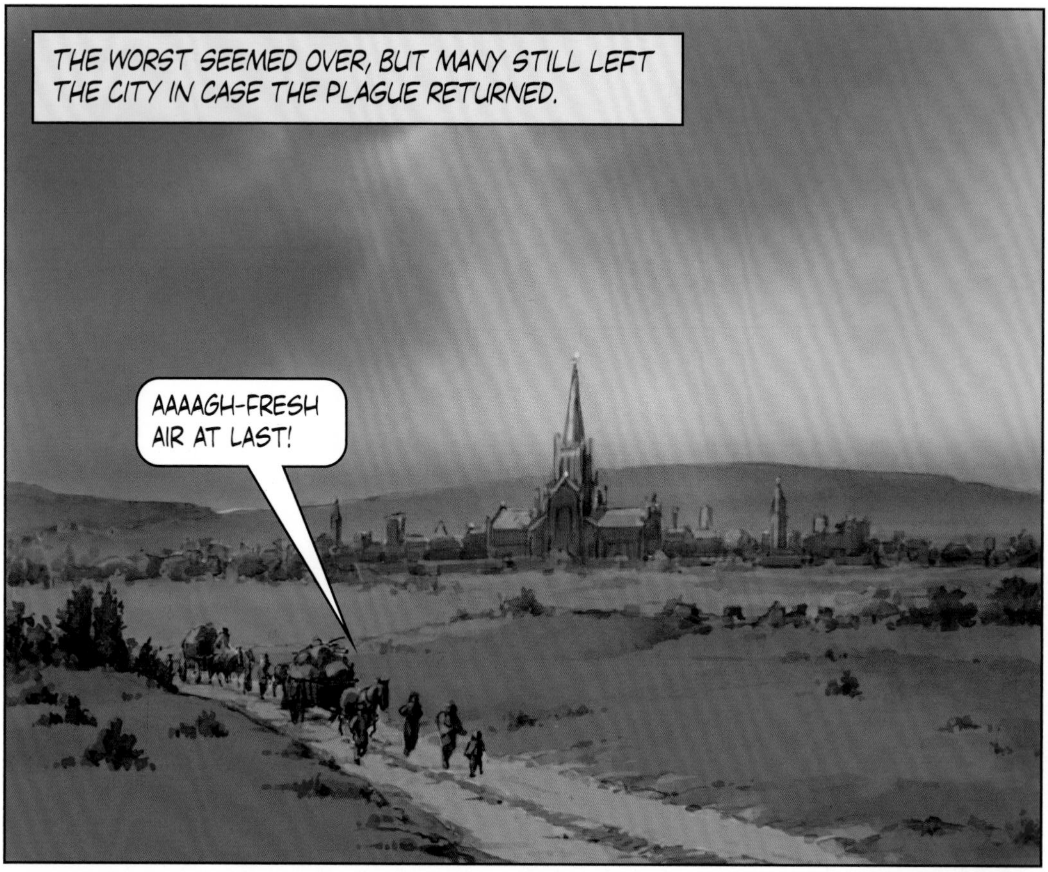
THE WORST SEEMED OVER, BUT MANY STILL LEFT THE CITY IN CASE THE PLAGUE RETURNED.
AAAAGH-FRESH AIR AT LAST!

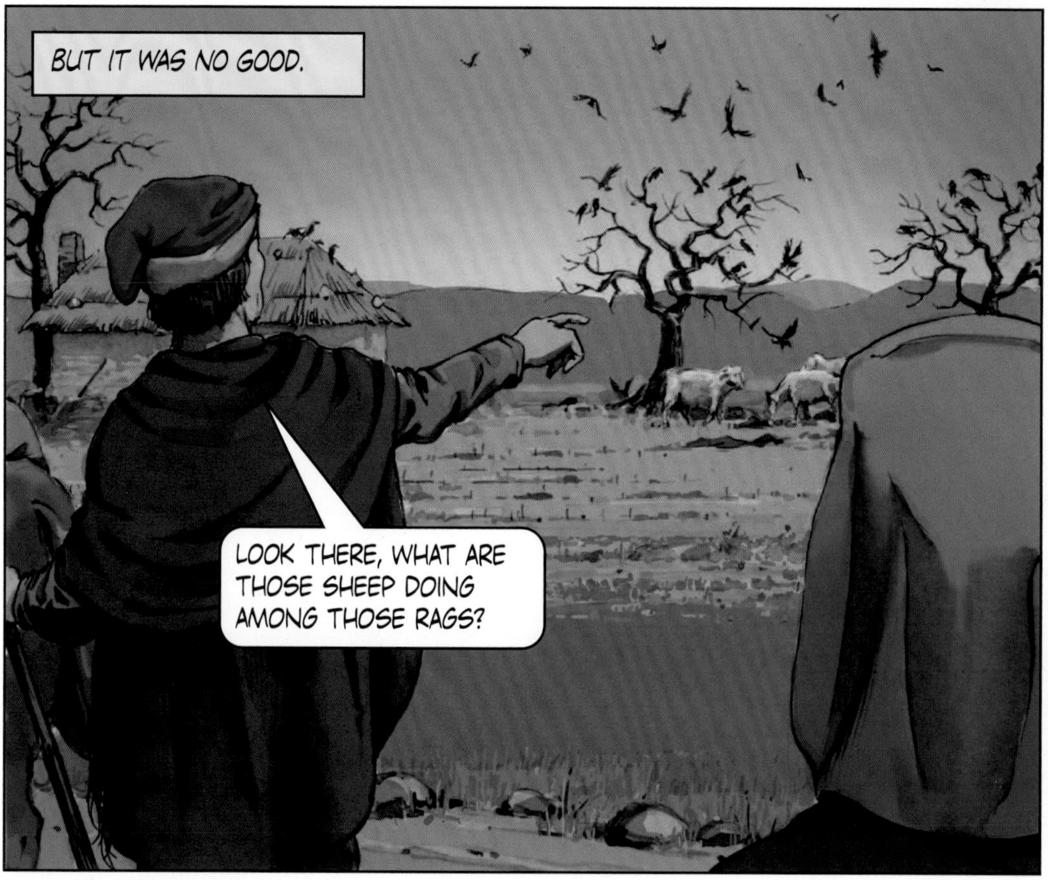
BUT IT WAS NO GOOD.
LOOK THERE, WHAT ARE THOSE SHEEP DOING AMONG THOSE RAGS?

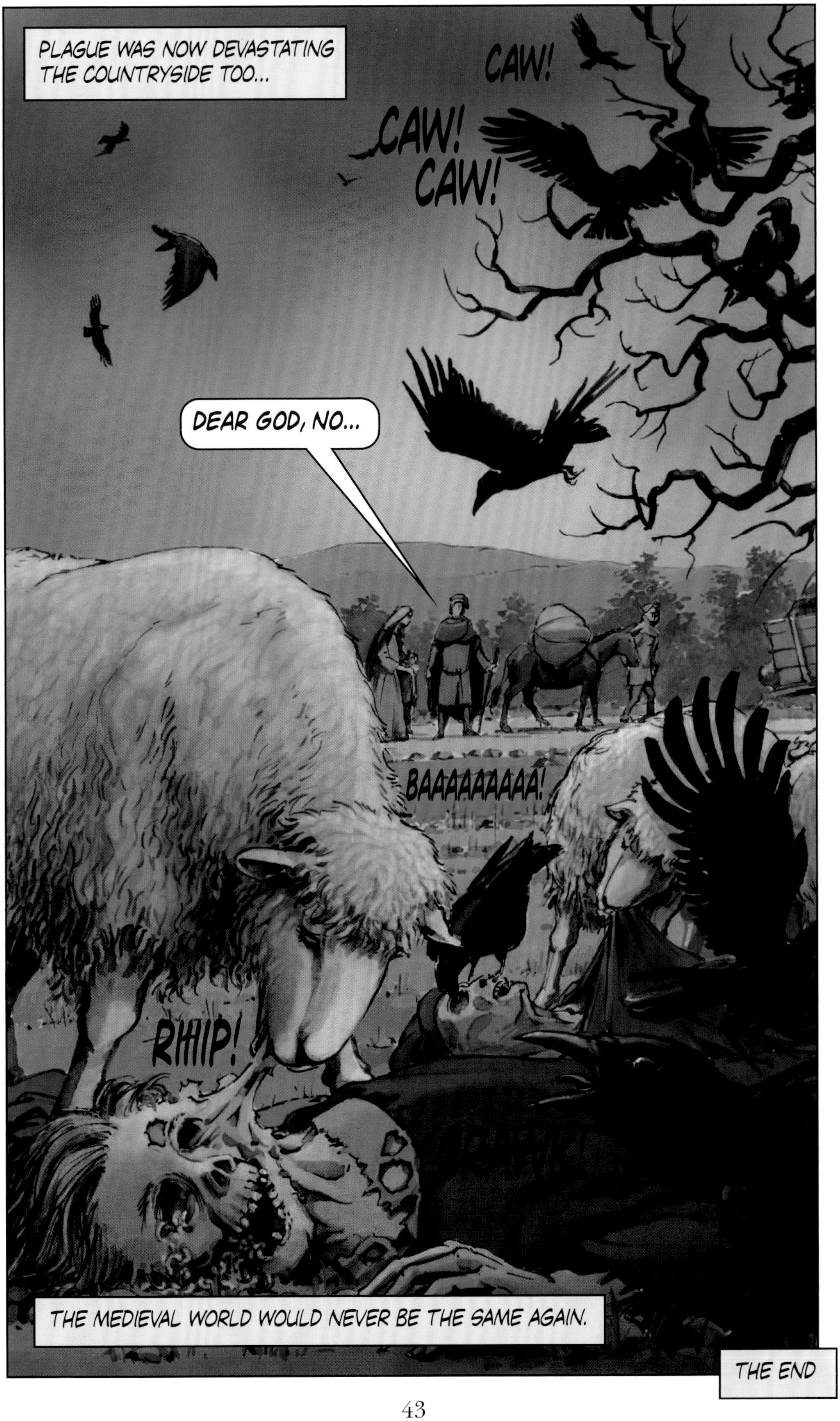
PLAGUE WAS NOW DEVASTATING THE COUNTRYSIDE TOO...
CAW!
CAW!
CAW!
DEAR GOD, NO...
BAAAAAAAAA!
RHIP!
THE MEDIEVAL WORLD WOULD NEVER BE THE SAME AGAIN.
THE END

After the Cataclysm

The Black Death killed between 75-200 million people over two years. Poor nutrition, bad hygiene, and overcrowding made the death toll worse among the peasants, but no one was safe—even royalty. Medieval plague cures were based on sniffing herbs, ancient medicine, and astrology.

Death would dominate art in the 15th century.

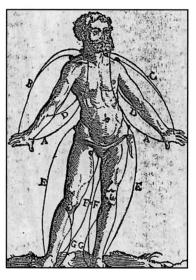

A 15th-century guide shows bloodletting points to "cure" the plague.

A Changed World

One immediate result of the Black Death was a long-lasting labor shortage.

In the feudal system, the lord of the manor "rented" a house and strips of land to a peasant to farm. These peasant tenants would "pay" him back by also farming the lands of the lord's manor, or estate. After 1350, with so many people wiped out, tenants were hard to come by. Rents paid to lords by tenants dropped. Fewer workers meant peasants suddenly had power to bargain for higher wages.

Popular Revolt

Governments across Europe reacted by freezing labor prices back to lower levels. Angry peasants wanted to be free to work for the highest bidder. Popular uprisings happened in many countries across Europe. Most were unsuccessful, but protests were the beginning of the end of the feudal system.

The English Peasants' Revolt of 1381 was caused by the farm laborers' desire to be free of the feudal system.

PLAGUE PERSISTS

Bubonic plague still exists. It regularly occurs in the fleas of rodents today. The Black Death pandemic happened because the disease jumped to humans when too many rats had died. Another species was needed to continue hosting it.

The outbreak ended when the plague had run its course, possibly because survivors had become immune, or the disease had weakened. But the plague was here to stay, living in rats until it became deadly enough to jump species again. Plague in Europe is rare today, as hygiene is understood, and we no longer live as close to vermin as medieval people did.

In Germany, this emblem would be displayed on the door of a house affected by the plague.

A 17th-century plague doctor (above) wears a nose piece containing smoking embers to ward off infection. The plague doctor at right has a beak mask stuffed with strong-smelling herbs. Even by the 17th century, the plague was still thought to be spread by "miasma," or bad air.

FURTHER PLAGUES

Plague outbreaks continued in Europe until the 1750s, but were never again as widespread as the Black Death.

One of the worst was the Great Plague of London in 1665. It killed over 100,000 of the people who lived in the filthy, overcrowded city.

Glossary

buboes Swollen, inflamed lymph nodes in the armpit or groin

bubonic plague Plague where buboes are common

calamity An event that causes great harm

cataclysm A large-scale disaster

contracted To become affected with; contract a cold

distinguished Widely known and admired for excellence

edifice A large, imposing building

epidemic A widespread occurrence of an infectious disease in a community at a particular time

extremity A limb or end part of the body, such as an arm or leg

feudal system The social system which developed in Europe in the 8th century

flagellant A person who subjects themselves or others to flogging, such as for religious discipline

fleam A handheld instrument used for bloodletting, or draining the blood

foregut The anterior part of the gut, toward the mouth

Gascony A region and former province of SW France, in the northern foothills of the Pyrenees. It was held by England between 1154 and 1453.

Golden Horde A Mongol and later Turkicized khanate, established in the 13th century, which comprised the northwestern sector of the Mongol Empire

groin The area between the abdomen and the upper thigh on either side of the body

heresy Opinion that is opposed to a generally accepted belief

holy ground An area recognized or declared sacred by a religion

humors Each of the four chief fluids of the body (blood, phlegm, yellow bile (choler), and black bile (melancholy) that were thought to determine a person's physical and mental qualities by the relative proportions in which they were present

illuminated manuscript A book, document, or piece of music written by hand, rather than typed or printed, and decorated with colorful illustrations

khanate A place ruled by a Khan or Khagan, the supreme rulers of the Turkish, Tartar, and Mongol peoples in the Middle Ages

lymph gland An oval-shaped organ of the immune system, situated throughout the body, including the armpit and stomach and linked by lymphatic vessels

immune Resistant to an infection

mayhem Needless or willful damage or violence

medieval Relating to the Middle Ages

moderately Neither very much nor very little: average in size or amount; neither very good nor very bad

morbid Gruesome or having a connection with death

mutated Changed or evolved in form or nature

pandemic A disease which is present throughout a whole country or the world

pestilence A fatal, large-scale disease

pneumonic Of, affecting, or relating to the lungs, or similar to pneumonia. "Pneumonic plague" affected the lungs.

porter A person employed to carry supplies

procession A number of people or vehicles moving forward in an orderly fashion, especially as part of a ceremony

prosperous Successful in material terms–flourishing financially

ravenous Extremely hungry

rodent A gnawing mammal, usually small, such as rats, mice, and squirrels

scholar A specialist in a particular branch of study, especially the humanities

septicemic plague A deadly infection affecting the blood; one of the three main forms of plague

swathe A broad strip or area of something

tenant A person who occupies land or property rented from a landlord

thong A thin strip of leather or hide

toxins Poisons or venom of plants or animals

vermin Wild animals which were believed to be harmful to crops, farm animals, or which carry disease

Index